LifeLog

A CELEBRATION OF THE

TWENTIETH CENTURY

Ben Haller

Miriam Bass

Kathleen Hughes

AnDex 2000 Los Angeles

To our loved ones, past and present,
Thank you for making this book possible and necessary.

The authors would like to thank Nancy McKinley, Susan Grode, Sue Olsen, Bob Zellin, Thom Dower, Kim Freilich, Irwin Friedland, Dianne Westpfahl, Francis Hobbs, Bob Martis, and everyone at Publishers Group West.

Researchers: Cary Martinez, Janet Sullivan, Henry Browne, and Lauren Arenson

Here's to the future: Geoffrey Allen, Heather, Maria Kovacs, Sam Arkush, Henry Anderson, Jess Munoz, Max Dower, Tularia Buttfield, Rudso, Max, Sara Bihn Brightman, Clem Healy, Nathaniel Paul Davis, Dylan, Kelsey and Hadley Kirkpatrick, Graham and Brian James Lesh, David, Alex, Creek, Christina, Shana, Sunshine, Anabelle, Theresa, Cassidy, Ambrosia, Lauren, Tony Elrick, Whip, Billy, Peggy, Jane, Justin, Bobby, Dick, Noah, Cory and Carly Steele, Alison, Michelle and Nick, Jesse and Jacob, Sam and Virginia, Dexter Gordon, Dinah Davison, Emily Beyda, and Tris and Toby.

CONTENTS

CONGRATULATIONS!

As the owner of a LIFELOG™, you are about to become part of history—a history in which you are a featured character. Your life will be highlighted against a fascinating backdrop of people and events. You can move through the years side by side with a fascinating group of people and events that we call the 20th Century.

Theodore Roosevelt refuses to shoot a bear cub while on a hunting trip in 1902, giving the world "Teddy Bears."

President Taft starts a baseball tradition by throwing out the first ball at a game in 1910.

Orson Welles scares America out of her wits with his *War of the Worlds* radio show on Halloween night 1938.

Neil Armstrong takes "one giant leap for mankind" as he steps onto the moon in 1969.

Chet Huntley signs off with his last "Goodnight David" in 1970.

Ads scream, "Where's the Beef?" and "Bet you can't eat just one."

The world breathes a great sigh of relief as the Cold War ends and the Berlin Wall comes tumbling down.

Interesting, but how do you fit in? Where were you? Where was your family?

WHAT WERE YOU DOING? Now you own a history book written for those of us who aren't included in more conventional volumes.

What was your first day of school like?

Who were your earliest playmates?

At 16, who was your favorite movie star?

At 18, what was your favorite song?

What was your first car?

To whom would you dedicate this book?

Where did your ancestors come from?

What would you like to tell your children and grandchildren?

If you were going to make a movie of your life,
    what actors would you choose to play the major roles?

Now you have a book that will answer all of these
    important questions.

NOW THAT YOU HAVE YOUR LIFELOG

LIFELOG has been created out of a need in our own lives. We find that no other book has the range of a LIFELOG. Baby books are too cute and don't cover enough ground. Diaries are inconvenient for scanning a number of years quickly. Appointment books and registers only cover one year. LIFELOG fills the void for us. We hope it will do the same for you.

If this book is for a child, the parents can make the early entries for the entire family. When children get older they will want to write their own history. What an wonderful gift you have chosen—one that will give a child both a record of the past and a feeling for the importance of self and family.

If this LIFELOG is a gift for an adult, it will show your appreciation to that person for a lifetime well spent and well remembered.

But wait! Most likely you bought the LIFELOG for yourself.

As a working person, the LIFELOG is needed to record jobs, credits, awards, and projects. As a family person, the LIFELOG is a treasured source for your roots. You may want to make it a tradition at family get-togethers to take out your book and make entries with the whole family.

Most likely, your life does not fill all the years of a LIFELOG. Don't worry. The object of this book is to get people to talk to one another. It will be a revelation to sit down with loved ones who have been through a world war, the Great Depression, or Vietnam and find out how it affected them. You will understand them better and you will have a written history—theirs and yours. They are the reason you are here. They are the reason you will cherish your LIFELOG.

For the years 1940 to 2000, we have included sections for headlines, songs, movies, and books. We've put items into those boxes, but we've also left room for your entries. Your personal headlines should be added to the headlines of the world. They belong there. What were your favorite movies and songs? What books did you enjoy? What news events affected you? WHAT WERE YOU DOING? LIFELOG is incomplete without you.

TO EVOKE A MEMORY

The entries at the top of each section are designed to stir your memory. The events, ideas, and people in LIFELOG have been assembled to evoke thoughts of times past. Some items appear when they were invented, published, or patented; others are entered when they became widely popular. We list people when they were best known. Births and deaths are included only when they, themselves, became important events. Sometimes a movie was not popular when it was released, but later came to stand for that era. Some patents, artists, and discoveries were never appreciated in their time. Now they are given the credit they deserve.

The LIFELOG is designed to trigger your memories. The pages are not full. We've started them. They must be completed by you.

One hundred years, it's all here between these covers. And remember, this is a book of participation. Write in the margins. Cross out things you don't like; add the things you do!

It's getting hard to tell the news from the history. A LIFELOG will give you a perspective as to where you stand. Interesting things don't happen in a vacuum. History is the relationship between you and what has happened in the world. Look at what joins us together. We have shared needs. That makes us human. We have shared memories. That makes for friends and family, tribes and nations. Knowledge and wisdom come when the memories help to solve and avoid problems in the present and future. A LIFELOG will help discover how the memories combine.

At the same time that Charles Lindbergh flew across the Atlantic, Babe Ruth was preparing to hit 60 home runs in one season and Al Jolson was warming up for his role in the 1st talking picture, *The Jazz Singer*. Chuck Yeager broke the sound barrier as Jackie Robinson was breaking into baseball. That year we were also watching Hope, Crosby, and Lamour in *The Road to Rio*. In just one year in another decade Americans were introduced to aluminum cans, felt tip pens, birth control pills, and the Bulova electronic watch. And later, while the Russians were sending the first man into space, we were establishing the Peace Corps. Time indeed produces some interesting combinations.

WHAT WAS I DOING? This is the question you will be asking yourself most often as you examine the pages of your LIFELOG. How do I combine with history?

SOME THOUGHTS ON HOW TO FILL IN YOUR LIFELOG

You have your whole life in front of you, so:

    Take your time.

    When in doubt, use a pencil.

    Learn to write small.

    And most important, have fun!

When filling in your LIFELOG, be inventive in finding sources. Now you can use those school yearbooks and company bulletins you've been saving. Your local library is always a good source. You can use the phone book, old travel diaries and maps, and local history books. But ultimately, the best place to go for information is the people you know—friends, co-workers, family.

THE YEARS 1900 TO 2000

The 21st century is upon us and those of us with our LIFELOGs will be prepared! The past is not important to some people, but you're different. This book will personalize the 20th century for you— with your needs, your dreams, and your memories. This will be the most fascinating history book you will ever read (or write)!

In LIFELOG, there is a space for every year from 1900 to 2000. There is always a place for you to write your own history next to what was happening in America. Before 1940, there are ten years to each two-page spread, with space left to write your memories. 1940 is the turning point. It marks the beginning of an incredible new time. From 1940 on, each year has its own two-page spread, again with room for you to fill in your own history. After 1989, you can continue to fill in world events along with your own accomplishments. Yes, there will be a LIFELOG for the 21st century. We will have one soon. For now, we welcome you as a "LifeLogger." Remember, the record you make here is YOU. Make it a challenge to fill it with wonderful memories and exciting adventures.

PERSONAL INFORMATION

Who were you named after?

It is important that you record the facts about yourself. Sometimes information gets lost. For your social security and passport numbers, contact the appropriate agencies. Look them up in the phone book under the proper United States Government offices or State offices. If you do not have a copy of your birth certificate, you can usually obtain one, for a small fee, by writing or calling the County Registrar's office where you were born.

The personal information section can also be used to record the events surrounding your birth. Were you born in a cab? Were you early? Was the doctor late?

There are two pages for notes after the Personal Information page. Wouldn't it be nice to have a note from your parents on the circumstances of your birth?

PRECAUTIONS AND PRIVACY

What was the most embarrassing thing you ever did?

Are you going to put it in your LIFELOG? Take care when writing in your book. It could be dynamite! Don't list your crimes, your one-night stands, or the times you lied. If your privacy is important to you, be careful about the entries and who sees them. You don't want to hurt someone who might read the book, including yourself. Be cautious about where you keep the book.

If you are concerned about the information in LIFELOG from a legal standpoint, you should consult an attorney. Laws differ from state to state and every person's needs are different. You must protect your privacy as you see fit.

FAMILY TREE

What is your favorite branch of the family?

We have designed a simple family tree. Change it or add to it as you see fit. Many of us have not traced our families back more than a generation or two. There are books in the reference sections of most bookstores and libraries about tracing your roots.

PERPETUAL CALENDAR

Why is Wednesday always the longest day of the week?

Here are the years from 1900 to 2000. You can look up any date in any year and find out exactly what day it will, or did, fall on.

Maybe you make your best business deals on Thursdays and you want to plan ahead for future ones. You might want to arrange your next wedding anniversary party early or turn an upcoming birthday into a long weekend.

BIRTHDAY/ANNIVERSARY CHART

Why do we keep adding more candles when each year we have less breath?

These pages are for every year, including leap years. Enter birthdays and anniversaries into the spaces. One look at the chart will tell you all of the critical dates coming up—what gifts, cards, flowers you have to send. You won't forget those very important days again.

PERSONAL CHRONOLOGY

In 1962 John F. Kennedy was President of the United States. The Cuban Missile Crisis and John Glenn's ride in space kept us aware of the excitement and dangers in the new technologies. At home the family dog was named Sam. In Congress, Sam Rayburn was Speaker of the House of Representatives. Our dog barked alot and made quite a fuss. He was the speaker of *our* house. We had a pony named Highball. She was white and her name had been Snowball, but her fondness for alcoholic drinks changed all that. I had a Classic 1931 Model A Ford I was trying to restore. My friends were Fred, Steve, Nadia, Joyce, and Al. These are some of the clues that bring back my memories of 1962.

Here is another way to look at the 20th Century. You can put together your own personal clues. Who were the friends that rode with you when you got your first car? What animal was the team mascot at your high school? What have been your golf scores over the years? What was the best secret hiding place you ever had?

You can customize this section to fit different needs. Maybe you have raised horses over the years. You can keep a list of the horses' names, shows, and ribbons in this section. Maybe you come from a family of baseball players. You can keep the family batting averages. Maybe you lived in New York City and never got a car. You won't need the section on cars, but you did take interesting vacations. What Broadway plays did you see?

Use the Personal Chronology for medical records. It is important to record shots, immunizations, and medical procedures. These records are an important part of your health history. This information could save your life. Talk to your parents to see if there are any conditions that run in your family. Many illnesses and conditions can be avoided by careful planning, diet, and knowledge.

INDEX

What year was the first Superbowl?

Here are the facts, names, and events of the 20th Century listed in alphabetical order. There are blank spaces at the end of every letter in the Index. You can add your important facts and dates to the Index as well as the individual years. Your important dates will be next to those we have included in LIFELOG. Marriages, births, graduations, and new jobs belong in your history of the 20th Century.

This is not a book of odd dates and obscure facts. LIFELOG doesn't list when something was first invented or when famous people were born. LIFELOG lists when events and people come into the public consciousness and will help us remember an era. The LIFELOG Index lists events as they appear in the book. Famous and not so famous people are listed by when we became aware of their exploits, not when they were born or died. TV shows are listed by the years they ran as first run and not when they were in syndication. Movies are listed by when they played in theaters and not when they were being written, shot, or became famous.

WHY DO WE NEED THIS BOOK?

America is no longer a sprawling young giant rushing to save the world in wars and then isolating herself in the vastness of her magnificent continent. The United States has become a mature country. We are the oldest democracy. Our great melting pot continues to swirl our many faces and voices together into one. We are a nation with a remarkable past and a great wealth of wisdom. While history is a great teacher, and it is very important to know the events, the dates, the people—this is not enough. We must know their relationship to us. With LIFELOG, we place our lives into the extraordinary framework that makes up America's 20th century.

We invite you to take a look at your life through a LIFELOG. These pages are meaningless without you. You couldn't have happened without history, and this history can't happen without you.

Pearl Harbor, John Glenn in space, Kennedy and Dallas, any World Series, Man on the Moon, the Space Shuttle disaster, and the smiling people atop the opened Berlin Wall: these are the hooks from which we hang history. These are the hooks for you to hang your history on in a LIFELOG.

Best of luck and happy memories with your LIFELOG!

THE
20TH
CENTURY

1900

American Baseball League • Casey Jones Dies in Train Wreck
In China the Boxer Rebellion Fights to Remove Western Influence
McKinley Beats Bryan for Presidency • *Sister Carrie*—Dreiser—Book
A Bird in a Gilded Cage—Song • Unskilled Labor Earns $2.50 Weekly
Sugar 4¢ lb, Eggs 14¢ doz, Butter 25¢ lb • 1st Davis Cup in Tennis

_____

_____

1901

Teddy Roosevelt Says, "speak softly and carry a big stick."
Spindletop Oil Field in Texas Begins to Gush • *Boola, Boola*—Song
McKinley Assassinated, Teddy Roosevelt Becomes President
The Settlement Cookbook proclaims, "the way to a man's heart...."
Captain Jinks of the Horse Marines—B'way • 1st Nobel Peace Prizes

_____

_____

1902

Teddy Bears: Roosevelt Won't Shoot Bear Cub on Hunting Trip
1st Rose Bowl, Michigan Beats Stanford • Dan Patch—Racehorse
Oliver Wendell Holmes Joins Supreme Court • Gibson Girls
Hound of the Baskervilles—Book • Marmon, Willys, Pierce, Overland—Cars
Bill Bailey Won't You Please Come Home—Song

_____

_____

1903

Wright Brothers Fly at Kitty Hawk • Cy Young Has Perfect Game
Typhoid Mary in New York City • 1st Ford Sells for $750
Boston Wins 1st World Series • *Ida Sweet as Apple Cider*—Song
Enrico Caruso Has 1st Million Seller • Iroquois Theater Fire, Chicago
Sweet Adeline—Song • *Call of the Wild*—Jack London—Book

_____

_____

1904

Louisiana Purchase Exposition St Louis-Hot Dogs & Ice Cream Cones
1st Olympic Games Held in US in St Louis, US Wins 21 Events
Rebecca of Sunnybrook Farm—Book • *The Cakewalk*—Dance Craze
NY Policeman Arrests Woman for Smoking in Public
Give My Regards to Broadway—Song • St Francis Hotel, San Francisco

_____

_____

_____

President's Conference in New Hampshire Ends Russo-Japanese War
Beginnings for Audubon Society, Rotary Club, and Caterpillar Tractors
Stanley Steamer Goes 127 MPH • 20th Century Limited—Train
Wait Til the Sun Shines Nellie & *My Gal Sal*—Songs
The Girl of the Golden West—B'way • Stereo Viewers—Fad

1905

Teddy Roosevelt 1st President to Travel Outside of USA
Nickelodeon Theaters Opening Everywhere • Corn Flakes Cereal
Roosevelt Gets Nobel Peace Prize for Ending Russo-Japanese War
You're a Grand Old Flag & *Anchors Aweigh*—Songs
San Francisco: Earthquake & Fire Destroy City • *The Jungle*—Book

1906

Oklahoma Becomes a State • 1st Mothers Day • *School Days*—Song
Panic on the Stock Market • 43,000 Cars Built This Year
Roosevelt and JP Morgan Hold Off Depression • Floradora Girls—Fad
President Sends US Fleet on Around-the-World Cruise
1st Ziegfield Follies Score by Victor Herbert • *Glow Worm*—Song

1907

Roosevelt Announces He Won't Run so Taft Wins the Election
Model T Ford, "stronger than a horse and easier to maintain," Costs $850
Jack Johnson Wins Heavyweight Crown • *Mutt & Jeff*—Comics
Take Me Out to the Ball Game—Song • *Wind in the Willows*—Book
Tinker to Evans to Chance • Isadora Duncan • Olympics in London

1908

Peary Claims to be 1st at the North Pole • *Three Lives*—Book
By the Light of the Silvery Moon—Song • Copyright Laws Pass Congress
Lincoln Head Penny Replaces Indian Head
Land Rush Begins as Taft Opens 700,000 Acres in West to Settlers
Women in Theater: Maxine Eliot, Ethel Barrymore, Julia Marlowe

1909

1910

Halley's Comet Reappears • Boy Scouts Chartered
The Average Man Earns $15 for a 60-Hour Work Week
Down by the Old Mill Stream—Song • *Naughty Marietta*—B'way
Carrie Nation Is Smashing Saloons for Prohibition
President Taft Starts Tradition—Throws Out 1st Ball for Baseball Season

1911

Wilson Sends Troops to Border to Protect Americans in Mexico
Cadillacs Have Electric Starters • Bestseller Books Cost $1.30
Fire in Triangle Shirtwaist Factory Exposes Sweatshop Conditions
Ty Cobb Bats .420 for Detroit Tigers • 1st Indy 500 Race
I Want a Girl Just Like the Girl That Married Dear Old Dad—Song

1912

Titanic Sinks in Atlantic, 1,513 Die • Jim Thorpe Wins at Olympics
New Mexico and Arizona Become 47th and 48th States
SOS Becomes Universal Distress Signal • *That Old Gal of Mine*—Song
Woodrow Wilson Beats Republican Taft and Bull Moose Roosevelt
Rules of Football Are Modernized to Give 6 Points for Touchdowns

1913

Vaudeville Thrives at The Palace • Federal Income Tax Becomes Law
Ballin' the Jack—Song • *Pollyana*—Book • *Perils of Pauline*—Movie
Mabel Norman Hits Ben Turpin with the 1st Custard Pie—Movies
The Armory Art Show Strengthens the Fine Arts in America
17th Amendment Has Senators Elected Directly by Voters

1914

World War I Begins, US Initially Declares Neutrality
You Can Have Any Color Model T Ford, As Long as It's Black
Penrod, Tarzan of the Apes & *. . . And a Far Country*—Books
Wrigley Field in Chicago and Yale Bowl Open for Sports Fans
Irene & Vernon Castle, Fred & Adele Astaire—Popular Dance Teams

The War Continues in Europe • Mata Hari Executed as a Spy
Wilson Sends Protest Notes to Germany Over *Lusitania* Sinking
Official Opening of Panama Canal Is Exposition in San Francisco
Song *Hello Frisco* Celebrates 1st Transcontinental Phone Lines
Birth of a Nation—Movie • *The Lone Star Ranger*—Book

1915

Wilson Sends Ultimatum to Germany Over Submarine Warfare
General Pershing Chases Pancho Villa After New Mexico Raids
Wilson's Campaign Slogan,"He Kept Us Out of the War"
I Ain't Got Nobody—Song • *Intolerance*—Movie • *Seventeen*—Book
America Doesn't Want to Go to War as Congress Warns "Don't Travel"

1916

Pershing Returns from Mexico • US Shows Zimmerman Telegram
Wilson,"The world must be made safe for democracy" • US Enters WW I
"Lafayette We Are Here" Pershing & Rainbow Division to France
Over There—Song • *Shoulder Arms*—Charlie Chaplin—Movie
US Population Passes 100 Million • "I Want You" Uncle Sam Poster

1917

Eddie Rickenbacker Becomes American Flying Ace
US Marines See Action in Belleau Wood • *Till We Meet Again*—Song
Pershing Now Commands 2 Million Troops • WW I Ends
Oh How I Hate to Get Up in the Morning—Song
Wilson Sails to Paris with His Fourteen Points for Peace

1918

Versailles Treaty Ends WW I • League of Nations Site to Be Geneva
Flappers Do the *Charleston* • *Sipping Cider Through a Straw*—Song
Jack Dempsey Heavyweight Champ • Father Divine Preaches
How Ya' Gonna Keep 'Em Down on the Farm—Song
While on Tour Promoting League of Nations, Wilson Suffers Stroke

1919

1920

Prohibition Becomes the Law • *Dr Jekyll and Mr Hyde*—Movie
US Attends Meeting of the League of Nations but Refuses to Join
Black Sox Baseball Scandal, "Say It Ain't So Joe" • Man o' War—Retires
Radio Station KDKA in Pittsburgh Begins To Broadcast
Women Get the Vote • Wilson Receives the Nobel Peace Prize

_____

_____

_____

1921

Congress Moves to Set Up General Accounting Office
Valentino—*The Sheik*—Movie Star • *The Sheik of Araby*—Song
Colonel Billy Mitchell Shows How Plane Can Sink Ship
End of War Brings Economic Hard Times, Wages Down, Hours Up
Armistice Day • Knee-length Skirts • *Main Street*—Book

_____

_____

_____

1922

20-Ton Meteorite Falls on Blackstone, Virginia • *Babbitt*—Book
500 Radio Stations Open Around Country • Buicks Get Heaters
Hollywood Scandals: Fatty Arbuckle & William Desmond Murder
Nanook of the North & *Orphans of the Storm*—Movies
The Blue Book of Social Usage—Emily Post—Etiquette

_____

_____

_____

1923

President Harding Dies and Calvin Coolidge Becomes President
Cars: Essex, Chandler, Dodge Brothers, Buick, Hupmobile, Maxwell
The Teapot Dome Oil Scandal Breaks in Congress • Strongheart—Dog Star
Yes We Have No Bananas—Song • US Steel Adopts 8-Hour Work Day
"Every Day in Every Way I Am Getting Better and Better"—Health Fad

_____

_____

_____

1924

"Keep Cool and Keep Coolidge"—Coolidge Wins Full Term
J Edgar Hoover Becomes Head of FBI • *It Had to Be You*—Song
Leopold and Loeb Sentenced to Life in Prison • *Tea for Two*—Song
Hollywood Names: Talmadge, Meighan, Gish, Tom Mix, DeMille
Mark Twain's *Autobiography*—Book • *The Student Prince*—B'way

_____

_____

_____

US Waits as Dog Sleds Race Diptheria Serum to Nome, Alaska
Millions Are Going to the Movies to See Disney Films, Chaplin, Valentino,
Paulette Goddard, Douglas Fairbanks, & Mary Pickford
Scopes Trial in Tennessee • Crossword Puzzles the Rage
Sweet Georgia Brown, If You Knew Suzie, & *Yes Sir! That's My Baby*—Songs

1925

Rudolph Valentino Dies • *Someone to Watch Over Me*—Song
Speed of Light Established at 186,284 Miles per Second
Gertrude Ederle is 1st Woman to Swim the English Channel
Millions Listen to Will Rogers on 1st NBC Radio Broadcast
The General—Buster Keaton • *The Sun Also Rises*—Hemingway—Book

1926

Babe Ruth Hits 60 Home Runs • Coolidge: "I Choose Not to Run"
Lindbergh Flies Atlantic in Spirit of St Louis
Sacco & Vanzetti Executed • Isadora Duncan Dies in Bugatti
The Jazz Singer—1st Talking Movie • *Elmer Gantry*—Book
Model A Ford Introduced • *Me and My Shadow*—Song

1927

Hoover Wins Presidency with "a Chicken in Every Pot"
Disney Releases *Steamboat Willie* with Mickey Mouse
Steamboat Bill Jr.—Movie • *Button Up Your Overcoat*—Song
The Flying Wallendas Join Ringling Brothers Circus • Penicillin
I Can't Give You Anything But Love, Baby—Song • Peanut Butter

1928

1st Academy Awards Presentations: *Wings, Sunrise,* & *Street Angel*
Paper Money Is Replaced by New Money ⅓ Smaller in Size
The Goldbergs Debuts on NBC Radio • St Valentines Day Massacre
Stock Market Crash, $30 Billion in Stocks Are Wiped Out
Tip Toe Through the Tulips & *Happy Days Are Here Again*—Songs

1929

1930

A New Planet Pluto Discovered • Judge Crater Disappears
Depression: 4.5 Million Unemployed and 1,300 Bank Closures
Animal Crackers—Marx Brothers • *The Blue Angel*—Marlene Dietrich
Chrysler Building • Irish Sweepstakes • Wood's *American Gothic*
Aimee Semple McPherson • Twinkies • *Blondie*—Comics • Airline Stewardesses

1931

Empire State Building Opens, the World's Highest • *Cimarron*—Movie
The Star-Spangled Banner Becomes the National Anthem
The Champ—Movie • *The Good Earth*—Book • *Dick Tracy*—Comics
Al Capone Goes to Jail for Tax Evasion • *Mood Indigo*—Song
Scottsboro Nine Arrested • Post and Gatty Fly Around the World

1932

Franklin Delano Roosevelt Elected Promising "New Deal"
Brother Can You Spare a Dime—Song • Lake Placid Winter Olympics
Lindbergh Baby Kidnapped • Bonus Army Visits Washington DC
Santa Claus Is Coming to Town—Song • *Brave New World*—Book
Depression Peaks: 34 Million Without Income, Average Salary $16 a Week

1933

FDR Sworn In, "The only thing we have to fear is fear itself"
Prohibition Ends • Chicago World's Fair Stars Sally Rand and Fans
Roosevelt Speaks to America in Fireside Chats on Radio
We're in the Money—Song • US Goes Off Gold Standard
Tom Mix Circus • *King Kong*—Movie • *Stormy Weather*—Song

1934

John Dillinger, Pretty Boy Floyd, Bonnie & Clyde Killed by G-Men
Many New Laws Help Control the Economy—SEC, FHA, FDIC
Monopoly—Game • *The Good Ship Lollypop*—Song • *Li'l Abner*—Comics
Chrysler Airflow Car Leads Way to Streamlining Automobiles
The Thin Man—Movie • *Life Begins at Forty*—Book • *Anything Goes*—Song

WPA Is Building a New America • FDR Signs Social Security into Law
Huey Long Assassinated in Louisiana • Paperback Books Selling Well
FDR Turns on Lights for Night Baseball, Crosley Field, Cincinnati
Chain Letter—Fad • *Begin the Beguine*—Song • *Top Hat*—Movie
Will Rogers Dies • *Lost Horizon*—Book • AA Founded

1935

Duke of Windsor Gives Up Throne for Love of Mrs Simpson
Baseball Hall of Fame Opens in Cooperstown, NY
Unemployment Insurance Begins with 1% Payroll Tax
Jitterbug—Dance • *I've Got You Under My Skin*—Song
Jesse Owens Wins 4 Gold Medals in Berlin Olympics • FDR Re-elected

1936

The Hindenburg Disaster Carried Live on Radio
FDR: "I see one third of a nation ill-housed, ill-clad, ill-nourished"
Golden Gate Bridge Opens in San Francisco • *My Funny Valentine*—Song
Amelia Earhart Disappears on Round-the-World Flight
How to Win Friends and Influence People—Dale Carnegie—Book

1937

On Halloween, Orson Welles' *War of the Worlds* Scares America
Joe Louis Beats Germany's Max Schmelling in 124 Seconds
Howard Hughes Flies Around the World in Record Time
Wrong Way Corrigan Flies to Ireland Instead of California
Lincoln Brigade • Trapp Family Singers Tour • *Bringing Up Baby*—Movie

1938

WW II Begins, US Stays Neutral • *Wizard of Oz*—Movie
Gone with the Wind Opens in Atlanta • *Beer Barrel Polka*—Song
FDR Declares National Emergency, Americans Told Not to Travel
Mr Smith Goes to Washington—Movie • *Day of the Locust*—Book
Goldfish Swallowing—Fad • Rollercoasters and Roller Rinks • DDT

1939

1940

JANUARY

FDR Submits $8.4 Billion Federal Budget
1st Social Security Checks Mailed • Nash Sedan $795
US Has 6 Million Farms and Exports 3 Million Tons of Wheat
I Hear a Rhapsody—Song • *Rebecca* & *Pinocchio*—Movies

FEBRUARY

30 Million Homes Have Radio
743 AM Stations in US • *Fibber McGee & Molly,
Your Hit Parade, The Quiz Kids, My Friend Irma,
The Jack Benny Show, Abbott and Costello,* & *The Shadow*—Radio

MARCH

Tokyo Olympics Canceled Due to War
Tommy Dorsey Plays • Big Band Era in Full Swing
France and Britain Agree No Separate Peace with Germany
Back in the Saddle Again—Gene Autry—Song • *Fantasia*—Movie

APRIL

Supreme Court Rules That Unions Can Picket and
That Federal Contractors Must Pay Minimum Wages
For Whom the Bell Tolls—Ernest Hemingway—Book
RCA Shows Electron Microscope • *Tuxedo Junction*—Song

MAY

Evacuation of Dunkirk • NY World's Fair Opens
Germans Reach English Channel
Sikorsky Stays Aloft for 1.5 Hours in Helicopter
"I have nothing . . . but blood, toil, tears, sweat"—Churchill—Radio

JUNE

Germans Invade France and Take Paris
The Last Time I Saw Paris & *Fools Rush In*—Songs
Mussolini Declares War on France and Britain
"This was their finest hour"—Churchill—Radio

HEADLINES

Hitler's Blitzkrieg Takes:
  France
  Belgium
  Holland
  Denmark
  Norway

FDR Re-elected

In England:
  Chamberlain Out
  Churchill Becomes
  Prime Minister

1940

JULY Supreme Court Rules That Records May Be Played on Radio
FDR Nominated for 3rd Term • Nylon Stockings
1st Revlon Lipsticks; Matching Lips and Fingertips
US to Build Planes for Britain: FDR Wants $4.8 Billion More for Defense

---

AUGUST Battle of Britain Begins • US Army Gets M & Ms
The Heart Is a Lonely Hunter—McCullers—Book
Gourmet Magazine and James Beard Start Food Careers
"We Want Wilkie" • US Imports 70% of World's Coffee Crop

SEPTEMBER FDR Embargoes Iron and Steel to All but Britain
Cabin in the Sky—Song • *The Thief of Baghdad*—Movie
England Gets 50 Used US Destroyers Under Lend-Lease Deal
16 Million American Men Will Register for Draft This Year

OCTOBER Peak Period for German U-Boat Successes
Cincinnati Over Detroit in World Series
40-Hour Work Week Goes into Effect • *San Antonio Rose*—Song
Kodak Flash for Cameras • The Army Gets 1st Jeep

NOVEMBER FDR Wins so John L Lewis Quits CIO as Promised
Ginger Rogers Gets Oscar for Movie Role in *Kitty Foyle*
Washington's Tacoma Bridge Falls into Puget Sound
Woody Herman, Sammy Kaye, Gene Krupa, Bob Crosby—Big Bands

DECEMBER FDR's Fireside Chat Calls US "arsenal of democracy"
US Industry Is Gearing Up for War Effort
Bears, Nagurski, and T-Formation Beat Redskins 73-0
The Time of Your Life—William Saroyan—Play • *Only Forever*—Bing Crosby

---

SONGS

*When You Wish
Upon a Star*
You Are My Sunshine
*Taking a Chance
on Love*
The Woodpecker Song

MOVIES

Road to Singapore
Philadelphia Story
Grapes of Wrath
The Great Dictator

BOOKS

Farewell My Lovely
The Ox-Bow Incident
*You Can't Go
Home Again*

1941

JANUARY

Congress Adjourns After 367 Day Session
FDR States Four Essential Freedoms for the World:
Freedom of Speech • Freedom of Worship
Freedom from Want • Freedom from Fear

FEBRUARY

Garbo Retires • German U-Boats Sink 39 Ships
Consolidated Aircraft Completes B-24 Bomber for RAF
Watch on the Rhine—Hellman • *Blithe Spirit*—Coward
& *Arsenic and Old Lace*—Kesselring—B'way Plays

HEADLINES

The War Rages
in Europe

Joe Di Maggio Hits in
56 Games Straight

Pearl Harbor

US Declares War
on Japan

US Declares War
on Germany

MARCH

National Gallery of Art Opens in Washington DC
Grand Coulee Dam Produces Its 1st Electricity
FDR Seizes German, Danish, and Italian Ships in US
Hudson, "America's Safest Car" • Plymouth $685 & Up

APRIL

FDR Seizes French Ships Including *Normandie*
FDR Proclaims National State of Emergency
Isolationist Lindbergh Quits Army Air Corps
Duffy's Tavern "Where the elite meet to eat"—CBS—Radio

MAY

Sculpture at Mount Rushmore Completed
German U-Boat Sinks US Ship *Robin Moore*
Parade Magazine Hits Newsstands • British Sink *Bismarck*
Artistry in Rhythm—Stan Kenton—Big Band • *The Fall of Paris*—Book

JUNE

Germany Declares War on Russia • FDR Promises Aid,
Freezes Italian and German Assets in US and Closes Embassies
Lili Marlene, Deep in the Heart of Texas, & *Blues in the Night*—Songs
German U-Boats Sink 61 Ships • *Amapola* & *Daddy*—Jimmy Dorsey

JULY

US Marines Protect Iceland • *Darkness at Noon*—Book
I Don't Want to Set the World on Fire—Song
Japanese Assets Frozen in US
MacArthur Put in Charge of US Forces in Far East

_____

_____

AUGUST

Service in US Army Extended to 18 Months
Gas Rationing on East Coast, Petroleum Exports Cut
World Population: 132 Billion, US: 133 Million
Lend a Paw—Disney Cartoon • *Sad Sack*—Comics

_____

_____

SEPTEMBER

US Diplomats Confer in Moscow
A Nightingale Sang in Berkley Square—Song
USS *Greer* Fights Off U-Boat with Depth Charges
Buckle Down Winsocki—Song • *Bulldog Drummond*—Radio

_____

_____

OCTOBER

Stan Musial Bats .426 for St Louis Cardinals
NY Yankees Beat Brooklyn Dodgers in Series
10% Excise Tax Placed on Luxury Goods
FDR on Radio: "America has been attacked; the shooting has started"

_____

_____

NOVEMBER

And Yet Americans Hope We Won't Go to War
Supreme Court Says California Cannot Stop People
from Migrating from Oklahoma • *Berlin Diary*—Book
Never Give a Sucker an Even Break—WC Fields—Movie

_____

_____

DECEMBER

Pearl Harbor Attacked by Japanese on the 7th

2,403 Men and 19 Ships Lost • Congress Votes to Go to War
90 Million Hear FDR on Radio: " a day that will live in infamy"

_____

_____

_____

1941

SONGS

Boogie-Woogie Bugle Boy
Take the "A" Train
Chattanooga Choo Choo

MOVIES

*How Green
    Was My Valley*
Citizen Kane
Sergeant York
Maltese Falcon
Sea Wolf

BOOKS

The Last Tycoon
*What Makes
    Sammy Run?*
*You Can't Do Business
    with Hitler*
*There Shall Be
    No Night*

1942

JANUARY

US Forces Retreating in Philippines
26 Nations Meet in DC, Agree to Fight Axis Powers
Ban on New Civilian Cars, No New Models Until 1946
All I Need Is You—Song • Rommel on Offensive in Africa

FEBRUARY

Britain and US Combine Chiefs of Staff
US Goes on Daylight Savings Time Until End of War
French Ship *Normandie* Burns in New York Harbor
Japanese Sub Shells Santa Barbara, Few Are Hurt

MARCH

100,000 "Nisei" Japanese Interred on West Coast
General MacArthur Leaves Manila for Australia
US Servicemen Get Free Mail Privileges
In the Blue of the Evening—Song • Carole Lombard Dies in Plane Crash

APRIL

Bataan Death March • Raisin Bran—Cereal
Edward Hopper Paints *Nighthawks*
General Jimmy Doolittle Leads US Bombers on Tokyo Raids
Blackouts on East Coast to Foil German Subs

MAY

Battle of Coral Sea; 1st Carriers and Planes
Sugar Rationing • Japanese Land on Corregidor
1,000 Allied Bombers Raid Cologne, Germany
FDR OKs Formation of WACs (Womans's Army Corp)

JUNE

The Battle of Midway • Rommel Takes Tobruk
FBI Gets German Spies Left by Subs in NY and Florida
1st Issue of *Yank* • Rudy Vallee Joins Coast Guard
Dwight David Eisenhower—US Commander in Europe

HEADLINES

Food and Gas
Rationing in US

Coconut Grove Fire
in Boston Nightclub

MacArthur;
"I shall return..."

War in Africa

War in Pacific

US Wins at Coral Sea
and Midway

1942

JULY

Gas Rationing, 3 Gallons a Week on East Coast
Henry J Kaiser Builds Liberty Ship in 10 Days
1st US Pilots Bomb Germany • *That Old Black Magic*—Song
Soldiers Love Canned Meat and Nylon Parachutes

_____

_____

AUGUST

Wendell Wilkie Tours World for FDR
1st All US Bombing Raid in Europe Over France
Americans Land in Guadalcanal • *Wabash Cannonball*—Song
Frank Sinatra Goes Solo, Leaving Tommy Dorsey Band

_____

_____

SEPTEMBER

Germans Reach Outskirts of Stalingrad
US Produced 488 Ships for War Effort in a Year
U-Boats Stalk Allied Convoys, Sinking 12, Losing 1 Sub
Praise the Lord and Pass the Ammunition—Song

_____

_____

OCTOBER

Glenn Miller Joins Army • *Woman of the Year*—Movie
US and Britain Promise to Investigate War Crimes
Tax Bill Puts Income Tax on Salaries Over $624 Yearly
Pacific Naval Battle Sees Carriers *Hornet* Sunk & *Enterprise* Damaged

_____

_____

NOVEMBER

Both Sides Have Lost 24 Ships at Guadalcanal
Draft Age Lowered to 18 • *Rodeo*—Aaron Copeland
Battle of El Alamein Has Germans and Italians in Retreat
Mrs Miniver—Movie • Ike Leads Invasion of North Africa

_____

_____

DECEMBER

Alcan Highway Links Alaska and Canada
Americans Tend Victory Gardens in Their Own Yards
Supreme Court Says Nevada Divorces Are Legal
Nuclear Reasearch Under Bleachers at Chicago University

_____

_____

SONGS

White Christmas
This Is the Army Mr Jones
You Made Me Love You
*You'd Be So Nice to
  Come Home to*

MOVIES

Yankee Doodle Dandy
  —Jimmy Cagney
Pride of the Yankees
  —Gary Cooper
Johnny Eager
  —Robert Taylor
Der Fueher's Face
  —Donald Duck

BOOKS

Song of Bernadette
Dragon Seed
*The Secret Life of
  Walter Mitty*
The Little Prince

1943

JANUARY

60,000 US Casualties in War So Far
Pentagon Completed in Arlington, Virginia
FDR and Churchill Meet in Casablanca
Mairzy Doats—Song • 1st All American Air Raid on Germany

HEADLINES

Allies Win in Africa

Allied Forces
Take Guadacanal

US Forces Island
Hopping in Pacific

Invasion of Italy

Germans Rescue
Mussolini

Oklahoma Opens
on B'way

FEBRUARY

Shoe Rationing • Salvage Drives Collect Tons of
Paper, Rubber, Steel, Iron, Tin Cans, and Newspaper
FDR Orders 48-Hour Work Week
Chevy Offers Blackout Special, No Chrome

MARCH

"Loose Lips Sink Ships", Germans Almost Defeat
Convoy System as U-Boats Sink 120 Allied Ships
Lassie Come Home—Movie • *I Can't Say No*—Song
This Month Men Ages 38-45 Allowed to Fight for US

APRIL

Meat and Cheese Rationing • *As Time Goes By*—Song
FDR Freezes Prices, Wages, and Taxes
FDR Dedicates Jefferson Memorial in Washington
Sliced Bread Banned to Save Money for War

MAY

US Troops Take Attu Island in the Aleutian Chain
Churchill Addresses Joint Session of Congress
FDR and Churchill Confer in Washington
Navy Says US Produced 700 Ships in 20 Weeks

JUNE

General De Gaulle Becomes Head of Free French
Don't Get Around Much Anymore—Song • Zoot Suits—Fad
Taxes Now Witheld from Paychecks • *God Is My Co-pilot*—Book
Americans Told: "Use it up, wear it out, make it do, or do without"

1943

JULY
Allied Troops Invade and Conquer Sicily
500 US Bombers Raid Targets Around Rome
Big Inch Pipeline Connects Texas and Pennsylvania
A Guy Named Joe—Movie • *Yankee Doodle Mouse*—Disney

AUGUST
Patton's Tanks Move Through Italy
American and Canadian Forces Take Back Aleutian Islands
Ending Threat of Japanese Invasion of US
Stage Door Canteen—Movie • B-29 "Superfortress"

SEPTEMBER
Allied Troops in 500 Ships Land at Salerno, Italy
People of Naples Now Fight Against the Germans
The Germans Rescue Mussolini from Italians
One for My Baby—Song • *This Is the Army*—Movie

OCTOBER
General Mark Clark Leads 5th Army into Naples
Fathers May Be Inducted into US Army
Italy Now Declares War on Germany
5th Army Moves Toward Rome • *Besame Mucho*—Song

NOVEMBER
US Troops Land on Solomon Islands
FDR and Churchill Meet Stalin in Tehran, Iran
Hey Good Lookin' & *I'm Popeye the Sailor Man*—Songs
The More the Merrier & *Shadow of a Doubt*—Movies

DECEMBER
US Seizes Railroads Due to Strike Threat
FDR's Christmas Radio Message; Eisenhower to Be
Supreme Allied Commander in Europe
German Navy Is Now Destroyed Except for U-Boats

SONGS

*Oh What a
Beautiful Morning*

*I've Heard
That Song Before*

*Comin' in on a Wing
and a Prayer*

He's My Guy

MOVIES

Casablanca
The Song of Bernadette
For Whom the Bell Tolls
Crash Dive

BOOKS

Here Is Your War
—Ernie Pyle

*A Tree Grows
in Brooklyn*

Dragons Teeth

*Our Hearts Were
Young and Gay*

1944

JANUARY

FDR's Budget $70 Billion, Mostly for War
Eisenhower Goes to London, Sets Up Headquarters
US Forces Invade Marshall Islands • *I'll Walk Alone*—Song
Allies Land at Anzio, Italy and Dig in • Spencer Tracy—Movie Star

FEBRUARY

Albie's Irish Rose & *Boston Blackie*—Radio
Wendell Wilkie Announces He Will Run
Anzio; Allied Invasion Stalls, Germans Take Initiative
Black Market Doing $1 Billion a Year Business

MARCH

This Month U-Boats Sink 54 Ships but Lose 60 Subs
I Couldn't Sleep a Wink Last Night—Song
Willie and Joe—GI Comic Strip • *Appalachian Spring*—Ballet
600 US Bombers Raid Berlin • Stalemate at Cassino, Italy

APRIL

Russians Win Back Odessa on the Black Sea
Allies Invade New Guinea in Pacific
MacArthur Says He Will Not Run for President
Accentuate the Positive—Song • Wilkie Withdraws

MAY

Allies Break Through at Cassino, Gustave Line Breaks
Meat Rationing Ends • *Laura*—Movie
U-Boats Sink Their Last Ship in Mediterranean
To Have or Have Not—Bogart and Bacall—Movie

JUNE

US 9th Army Captures Rome • GI Bill of Rights
D-Day Invasion of Normandy with 1st Army, 3rd Army,
7th Army, Omaha, Utah, Juno, Gold, and Sword
1st V1 Rockets Hit England • Battle of Phillipine Sea

1944

JULY   FDR Nominated • Attempted Assassination of Hitler
GOP Nominates Dewey • Doz Eggs 64¢, Steak 45¢ lb
Patton's Tanks Drive Through France to Germany
Ringling Circus Tent Burns in Hartford, Connecticut, 168 Die

_____

_____

AUGUST   General "Vinegar Joe" Stillwell Leads US-China Forces
US Forces Take Guam • *Pistol Packin' Mama*—Song
General LeClerc Leads French Troops into Paris
De Gaulle Returns Soon After • *Up in Arms*—Movie

_____

_____

_____

SEPTEMBER   US Troops Enter Germany
Hurricane Kills 400 on US East Coast
British Troops Enter Brussels • 1st V2 Rockets Hit Britain
Let's Re Re Re Elect Roosevelt—Campaign Song

_____

_____

OCTOBER   Churchill and Eden Visit Stalin in Moscow
Allies Attack Formosa • Warsaw Uprising
Japan Loses 24 Ships in Battle of Leyte Gulf
MacArthur Fulfills Promise, "I Have Returned"

_____

_____

NOVEMBER   British Bombers Find and Sink German
Battleship *Tirpitz* Hiding in Norwegian Fjord
FDR Wins 4th Term • *Thirty Seconds Over Tokyo*—Movie
Harry S Truman—Vice President • *There I've Said It Again*—Song

_____

_____

DECEMBER   Glenn Miller's Plane Lost Over Europe
George Marshall, Eisenhower, MacArthur, and
Hap Arnold Are Made 5 Star Generals • Battle of the Bulge
US General MacAuliffe Says "Nuts" to German Surrender Demand

_____

_____

_____

SONGS

Don't Fence Me in
Rum and Coca Cola
Swinging on a Star

MOVIES

Going My Way
Meet Me in St Louis
Curse of the Cat People
Since You Went Away

BOOKS

The Lost Weekend
A Bell for Adano
Razor's Edge
I Never Left Home
*Anna and
    the King of Siam*

1945

JANUARY

Frozen Dinners Are Offered on Airlines
USS *Boise* with MacArthur Aboard Almost Sinks in
the Battle for Luzon in the Pacific
Patton Crosses into Germany Taking Oberhausen

_____

_____

_____

FEBRUARY

1,000 US Bombers Raid Berlin • *Laura*—Song
The Yalta Conference, Churchill, FDR, Stalin
Allied Troops Reach Rhine River
Fighting Ends on Corregidor • *State Fair*—Movie

_____

_____

_____

HEADLINES

VE Day

FDR Dies,
  Truman President

Germany Surrenders

The A Bomb

VJ Day,
  Japan Surrenders

Hitler and Mussolini
  Dead

MARCH

The Great Gildersleeve, Superman, The Green Hornet,
Inner Sanctum, Fred Allen's Alley, One Man's Family,
Queen for a Day , & *Red Ryder*—Popular Radio
Allies Reach Bridge at Remagen • US Forces Take Iwo Jima

_____

_____

_____

APRIL

FDR Dies, Harry S Truman Becomes President
Nazi Concentration Camps Discovered by Allies
Ernie Pyle War Correspondent Dies in Pacific
US Forces Invade Okinawa • *The Story of GI Joe*—Movie

_____

_____

_____

MAY

American Troops Ordered Not to Enter Berlin
2 Million German Troops Surrender
Germans Sign Unconditional Surrender
Carrier *Bunker Hill* Attacked by Kamikaze

_____

_____

_____

JUNE

Fighting Ends on Okinawa • *Mildred Pierce*—Movie
Perry Como, Dick Hymes, Jo Stafford,
Helen O'Connell, Kay Starr, Bob Crosby, Orrin Tucker,
Skinnay Ennis, Hoagy Carmicheal—American Musicians

_____

_____

_____

1945

JULY
Churchill Loses Election in England
Truman Establishes the Medal of Freedom
B-25 Bomber Hits Empire State Building
Berlin Is Divided Into Sectors • *Till the End of Time*—Song

AUGUST
B-29 Drops Atomic Bombs on Hiroshima and Nagasaki
Fluoridation of Water Begins in Grand Rapids, Michigan
Allied Forces Total Liberation of the Phillipines
Korea Divided at the 38th Parallel • *Rhapsody in Blue*—George Gershwin

SEPTEMBER
Anchors Aweigh & *National Velvet*—Movies
Allies Meet in London to Draw Up Peace for Europe
Japan Surrenders Aboard USS *Missouri*
MacArthur Made Supreme Commander, Occupies Japan

OCTOBER
29 Nations Ratify the UN • *Sioux City Sue*—Song
Ball Point Pens Go on Sale at Gimbles, NY for $12.50
Shoe Rationing Ends • Black Market Thrives
Glass Menagerie—Play • *Carousel*—Musical

NOVEMBER
Nuremburg War Crimes Trials Begin
Ike Replaces Marshall as Army Chief of Staff
Meat and Butter Rationing Ends • Del Webb Buys Yankees
Coke Is Registered as a Trademark • *Give Me the Simple Life*—Song

DECEMBER
I'm Beginning to See the Light—Song
Senate OKs US Joining UN • *Beyond the Sea*—Song
Patton, Removed from Control of 3rd Army, Dies After Car Wreck
General Marshall Tries for Peace Between Chinese Factions

SONGS
*Kiss Me Once
Kiss Me Twice*
Personality
*You'll Never
Walk Alone*

MOVIES
The Lost Weekend
The Bells of St Marys
*A Tree Grows
in Brooklyn*

BOOKS
The Black Rose
Immortal Wife
Black Boy
Cannery Row
The Open Society
Animal Farm

1946

JANUARY

US Sole Trustee of Islands Taken from Japan
Truman Asks Public to Help Peacetime Economy
London Hosts the 1st Session of the United Nations
Truman Creates the CIA Headed by "Wild Bill" Donovan

HEADLINES

UN 1st Session
Accepts Land in
New York City

"An Iron Curtain"
Falls Across Europe
—Churchill

Chinese Civil War
Resumes

Labor Strikes Plague
Many Industries

Flamingo Hotel Opens
in Las Vegas

FEBRUARY

Truman Brings Price and Wage Deregulation
"Go Nash and Save Money Every Mile"
"There's a Ford in Your Future" • "8 out of 10 Say DeSoto Again"
Ranch Style Homes • US Births Begin to Soar

MARCH

Gilda, The Big Sleep, Blue Skies, & *Cat Concerto*—Movies
Americans Eat Less to Help a Starving World
United Auto Workers Strike Successful, 18½¢ Raise
Supreme Court Bans Segregation on Interstate Buses

APRIL

400,000 Mine Workers Go on Strike • NBC TV News
Farm Prices at Record High • Roosevelt Dime
To Each His Own—Song • *Duel in the Sun*—Movie
War Crimes Trials Tokyo • *Annie Get Your Gun*—B'way

MAY

Marines Put Down Alcatraz Prison Riot
18 to 19 Year Olds and Fathers Exempt from Draft
Strikes: US Troops Seize Railroads and Coal Mines
On the Atchison, Topeka, and the Santa Fe—Song

JUNE

Baruch Submits US Atomic Energy Plan to UN
US Joins UNESCO • *The Yearling*—Disney—Movie
*Doctor, Lawyer, Indian Chief, Old Devil Moon,
I'm Always Chasing Rainbows,* & *One-zy, Two-zy*—Songs

1946

JULY

Atomic Testing Begins on Bikini Island
The Phillipines Independent After 48 Years
Truman Extends Price Controls Another Year
In All-Star Game, Ted Williams Drives in 9 Runs

AUGUST

Atomic Energy Commission Put Under Civilian Control
Senate OKs World Court • National School Lunch Act
Truman Signs $2 Billion for Departing Servicemen
Ole Buttermilk Sky—Hoagy Carmichael—Song

SEPTEMBER

Britain Gives India Independence
Nuremburg Trial Verdicts • Lucky Luciano Deported
Family Circle—Magazine • *The Old Lamplighter*—Song
Red Tide Spoils Florida Beaches • *All the King's Men*—Book

OCTOBER

US Will Keep Troops in South Korea to Keep It Free
Truman Lifts Meat Price Controls • *I the Jury*—Book
Louis–Conn Fight on TV, Cards Over Red Sox in Series
Glen Davis and Doc Blanchard, Chicago Bears—Sports

NOVEMBER

Truman Rides in Captured German Sub in Naval
Maneuvers off Florida • Jukeboxes Are the Rage
Coal Miner's John L Lewis Fined $3.5 Million for Strike
Republicans Take Control of the House and Senate

DECEMBER

Fire in Winecoff Hotel in Atlanta, 127 Die
New in the Stores: Tide Detergent, Beautiful Hair Breck,
Holiday Magazine, Timex Watches, French's
Instant Potatoes, Packard Deluxe Clipper $1,746

SONGS

Tenderly

*Anything You Can Do
I Can Do Better*

*There's No Business
Like Show Business*

*Come Rain or
Come Shine*

Surrender

MOVIES

It's a Wonderful Life

*The Best Years
of Our Lives*

Notorious

My Darling Clementine

BOOKS

All the King's Men

*A Member of
the Wedding*

This Side of Innocence

1947

JANUARY
Truman's Budget $37 Billion • *Too Fat Polka*—Song
The Bachelor and the Bobbysoxer—Cary Grant—Movie
Smoke, Smoke, Smoke—Song • *Green Dolphin Street*—Movie
All My Sons—Arthur Miller—Play • *The Harder They Fall*—Book

FEBRUARY
Voice of America Begins Broadcasting
Everglades National Park Established in Florida
5¢ Hershey Bar • Almond Joy Bar • Reddi Whip
Eames Chair • Frozen Orange Juice • Tubeless Tires

MARCH
The Ghost and Mrs Muir—Movie
New York Transit Fares Go From 5¢ to 10¢
US Gets 99 Year Leases on Phillipine Bases
Congress Ends Draft and Pushes Presidential Two-Term Amendment

APRIL
Henry Ford Leaves $625 Million to Ford Foundation
Jackie Robinson Signs with Brooklyn Dodgers
Babe Ruth Tells Crowd Good-bye at Yankee Stadium
Body and Soul—Movie • *Golden Earrings*—Song

MAY
Willie Sutton—Robber • *Under the Volcano*—Book
Truman Gets $350 Million for War-torn Europe
Kraft Television Theatre • Cadillac: "The Standard of the World"
Dodge: "Smoothest Car Afloat" • Lincoln: "Nothing Could Be Finer"

JUNE
Round the World Ticket on Pan AmCosts $1,700
The Marshall Plan for Europe's Recovery
Congress Passes Taft-Hartley Over Truman's Veto
Army Gives Back Coal Mines after Strike Seizure

HEADLINES

Chuck Yeager Breaks
Sound Barrier

Jackie Robinson
Plays Baseball

Kon Tiki Sails Pacific

Dead Sea Scrolls

The Marshall Plan

Taft-Hartley Act Passed

Yankees Win 1st TV
World Series

1947

JULY
Peg O' My Heart—Song • Albert Schweitzer in Africa
Hoover Commission Looks at the Government
US Has Sent 18 Million Tons of Food Overseas
Brigadoon—B'way • *The Farmer's Daughter*—Movie

AUGUST
US Pilot Flies Round World in 73 Hours 5 Min 11 Sec
Shoe Shine—Movie • *Lucifer*—Jackson Pollock—Painting
Flying Saucers Reports • Christian Dior Lowers Hemlines
For Sentimental Reasons—Song • *Finian's Rainbow*—B'way

SEPTEMBER
I Wonder Who's Kissing Her Now?—Song
James Forrestal Becomes 1st Secretary of Defense
Columbia Breaks Army Unbeaten Football String at 32 Games
Bar Harbor, Maine Fire—Disaster Area

OCTOBER
Chuck Yeager Breaks Sound Barrier in Bell X-1
Johnny Lujac, John Cobb, Yankees, Dodgers
Notre Dame, Jack Kramer, Ben Hogan
Chicago Cardinals, Al Gionfriddo, Leo Durocher—Sports

NOVEMBER
UN Calls for Jewish State in Palestine
Howard Hughes Flies *Spruce Goose* 1 Mile
Truman Asks for $597 Million Foreign Aid
Hollywood Blacklist: "10" Refuse to Testify for Congress

DECEMBER
25-Inch Snowfall Kills 80 in New York City
The Road to Rio—Hope, Lamour, Crosby—Movie
Accent—Seasoning • *Cyrano de Bergerac*—José Ferrer—B'way
A Streetcar Named Desire—Tennesse Williams Play Opens in New Orleans

SONGS

Ivy
Zip-A-Dee-Doo-Dah
Open the Door Richard
Almost Like
    Falling in Love

MOVIES

Miracle on 34th Street
Great Expectations
Life with Father
Forever Amber

BOOKS

The Diary of
    Anne Frank
Tales of the
    South Pacific
The Egg and I
Gentleman's Agreement
Information Please
    Almanac-1947

1948

JANUARY

Congress Decides to Fund *Voice of America*
Ted Mack Original Amateur Hour—DuMont Network
Gateway Arch—St Louis • *Kiss Me Kate*—Musical
Christina's World—Andrew Wyeth—Painting • Dial Soap

HEADLINES

Truman Elected

The Olympic
  Games Resume

Berlin Blockade
  by USSR

Gandhi Assassinated

Isreal Created by UN

Polio Epidemic

The Cold War

Transistor from
  Bell Labs

FEBRUARY

Truman Sends Civil Rights Legislation to Congress
Ike Retires from Army to Head Columbia University
Air Force Project Bluebook Looks at Flying Saucers
Margaret Sanger Starts Planned Parenthood

MARCH

It's Magic—Doris Day, *Nature Boy,* &
All I Want for Christmas Is My Two Front Teeth—Music
The Supreme Court Rules Against Religious Training in Public Schools
Arturo Toscanini and NBC Symphony from Carnegie Hall—TV Debut

---

APRIL

Soviets Begin to Blockade Allied Parts of Berlin
Gas 25¢ a Gallon • Daily Paper 3¢ • Blue Jeans $3.45
1st Long-Playing Records from Columbia at 33 ⅓ RPM
Nestle's Quik • Teflon • *Easter Parade*—Movie

MAY

North Korea Goes Communist • *CBS TV News*
United Auto Workers Get Cost-of-Living Clause
Johnny Belinda, Red River, Sorry Wrong Number,
The Bicycle Thief, I Remember Mama, & *The Red Shoes*—Movies

JUNE

Bill Boyd Is *Hopalong Cassidy* on NBC TV
Mt Palomar, World's Largest Telescope, California
Republicans Nominate Dewey • *Candy Kisses*—Song
The Treasure of Sierra Madre—Bogart and Houston—Movie

1948

JULY — Dixiecrats Walk from Convention as Democrats Nominate Truman with Civil Rights Plank
Candid Camera—TV • Truman Bars Segregation in Armed Forces
President Dedicates New York's Idlewild Airport

AUGUST — *America's Town Meeting of the Air*—TV Show
I'm Looking Over a Four Leaf Clover—Song
Chambers and Nixon Go After Hiss as Communist
US Is Unofficial Winner of London Olympics with 35 Gold Medals

---

SEPTEMBER — "Nobody Wants War, Harry Truman Knows Why"
"Depend on Dewey" • North Koreans Want All of Korea
Fort Apache—Movie • Railroads Switching Coal to Diesel
Netherlands' Queen Gives Crown to Daughter Juliana

OCTOBER — *Philco Playhouse*—TV • *Now Is the Hour*—Song
Lou Boudreau, Doak Walker, Cleveland Indians,
Pancho Gonzales, Eddie Arcaro, Citation—Sports
Bernard Baruch Warns: "We are in a cold war, getting warmer"

NOVEMBER — Chicago Headlines Announce Dewey Winner
Truman Wins, Democrats Win Control of Congress
In LA, Madman Muntz Sells 4,500 TVs a Weekend
1 Million Homes Have TVs • *Buttons and Bows*—Song

DECEMBER — Packard: "Ask a Man That Owns One"
Tojo and 6 Others Hung in Tokyo for War Crimes
Truman Extends Rent Controls • Philadelphia Eagles—Football
Arthur Godfrey's Talent Scouts—TV • Walter Winchell Rated #1

SONGS

*I'll Be Home
for Christmas*

*On a Slow Boat
to China*

Sleigh Ride

Ballerina

MOVIES

Key Largo
A Letter to Three Wives
Hamlet—Olivier
The Pirate

BOOKS

*The Naked and
the Dead*

*Cry the
Beloved Country*

The Loved One

The Young Lions

Raintree County

1949

JANUARY

The Goldbergs—America's 1st TV Sitcom
Congress Raises the President's Salary to $100,000
Our Miss Brooks & *The Bob and Ray Show*—Radio
Sam Rayburn, Texas—Speaker of the House • *Mule Train*—Song

FEBRUARY

Film Star Robert Mitchum Busted for Pot
GM Drops Car Prices So Auto Workers Drop Wages
Chevrolet $1,339 • Cadillac $2,840
Revlon Introduces Fire and Ice with Suzy Parker

MARCH

Mama, Stop the Music & *We the People*—TV
Dean Acheson Replaces Marshall as Secretary of State
Suspense—1st TV Thriller Series • *So in Love*—Song
French Are Opposed by Ho Chi Minh in Vietnam

APRIL

NATO: 12 Nations Form North Atlantic Treaty Organization
US, Britain, and France Merge Their Berlin Sectors
1,000 Convictions in Nuremburg War Crimes Trials
Mayo Clinic Manufactures Cortisone

MAY

Soviets Lift Berlin Blockade • *South Pacific*—B'way
General Mills and Pillsbury Have Prepared Cake Mixes
RCA Sells 7" 45 RPM Records • *Bonaparte's Retreat*—Song
Some Enchanted Evening—Song • *Death of a Salesman*—Play

JUNE

US Troops Leave Korea • *For Me and My Gal*—Song
Supreme Court Says DAs May Use Illegal Evidence
Joe Louis Retires • *White Heat*—Jimmy Cagney—Movie
Ezzard Charles Beats Jersey Joe Walcott for Boxing Crown

HEADLINES

NATO Formed

Mao Leads Communists
to Victory in China

Chiang Kai-shek
Moves to Formosa

Russia Gets A-Bomb

Macy's and Gimbel's
Fight Over Polaroid
Cameras

1949

JULY   Congress OKs NATO • Truman Asks for $1.4 Billion Aid
Tokyo Rose Goes on Trial in San Francisco
Friday Night Frolics—Sid Caesar and Imogene Coca—TV
Marge and Gower Champion • Dow Jones Average 161

AUGUST   Truman Signs National Security Act: Sec Army
Sec Navy,   Sec Airforce Now Cabinet Level
General Omar Bradley, Chairman Joint Chiefs of Staff
FCC Bans Giveaway Shows on Radio as Gambling

SEPTEMBER   Philip Johnson Glass House, Connecticut
26-Story John Hancock Building Goes Up in Boston
Jack Benny & *Amos and Andy* on Sundays—CBS Radio
Truman Announces USSR Has Bomb • *Lone Ranger*—TV

OCTOBER   500,000 Steel Workers Go on Strike
US Still Refuses to Recognize Red China
UN Headquarters Dedicated in New York
Life of Riley—William Bendix—TV • Yankees Beat Dodgers

NOVEMBER   P-38 Fighter Hits Passenger DC-4 Near Washington
General Motors Made $500 Million So Far This Year
US Fires 2 Stage Rocket 244 Miles at White Sands
Adam's Rib—Movie • Sara Lee Cheesecake • Silly Putty

DECEMBER   *Rudolph the Red-Nosed Reindeer*—Song
1st Emmy Awards • Chicago O'Hare Airport Opens
Uncle Milty on TV • Chiang Kai-shek Completes Move to Formosa
Time Magazine Man of the ½ Century: Churchill

SONGS

The Harry Lime Theme
Baby It's Cold Outside
That Lucky Old Sun
Mockin' Bird Hill

MOVIES

The Third Man
On the Town
Twelve O'Clock High
The Heiress

BOOKS

1984
Cheaper by the Dozen
*The Greatest Story
Ever Told*
The Lottery
The Fireside Cookbook

1950

HEADLINES

Korean War Starts

Inchon Invasion

Puerto Rican
Nationalists Try
to Kill Truman

Brinks Robbery Nets
Over Two Million

Allies Let Germany
Rearm

JANUARY

Truman's Budget $42.4 Billion, ⅓ for Defense
Masked Robbers Hit Boston Brinks for $2.7 Million
In 2nd Trial, Alger Hiss Found Guilty, Gets 5 Years
Truman Says US Will Build Hydrogen Bomb

FEBRUARY

What's My Line?—TV • *Mona Lisa*—Song
Guys and Dolls—B'way • *A Town Like Alice*—Book
Joe McCarthy Shows List and Says State Dept Hides Commies
US and Canada to Work Together on Niagara Falls

MARCH

Berkeley Scientists Have New Element, Californium
1 Car for Every 3.5 Americans, 40 Million Cars
Birdland Opens in NYC with Charlie Parker
FBI Issues the 1st 10 Most Wanted Criminals List

APRIL

Soviets Shoot Down US Plane Over Baltic Sea
Supreme Court Backs HUAC's Forcing Testimony
Truman Signs Bill; Hopi and Navajo Get $10 Million
Rag Mop, My Foolish Heart, & *Enjoy Yourself*—Songs

MAY

Acheson Announces US Aid to French in Vietnam
Jimmy Stewart & Invisible Rabbit Star in *Harvey*—Movie
Truman Opens Grand Coulee Dam in Washington State
Kefauver Crime Commission Hearings in Miami

JUNE

North Korean Troops Invade Across 38th Parallel
Truman Authorizes US Troops to Korea
US Gets Soviets to Walk Out of UN, Then Gets Vote
to Send UN Troops to Korea • Communists Take Seoul

1950

JULY
MacArthur Becomes UN Commander in Korea
Truman Asks for $20 Billion for Rearmament
Panic in the Streets, Rio Grande, & *Wagonmaster*—Movies
Cherry Pink and Apple Blossom White—Song

AUGUST
Army Calls Up 62,000 Reservists
US Defeats USSR Bid to Get Red China Into UN
9 Million Additional Qualify for Social Security
Smokey the Bear Symbol of Forest Fire Prevention

SEPTEMBER
North Koreans Are Doing Well in War Until
UN Troops Land at Inchon, Recapture Seoul,
Then Drive Communists Back to 38th Parallel
McCarren Act Makes Communists Register in the US

OCTOBER
MacArthur Crosses 38th Parallel Into North Korea, Then
Meets with Truman on Wake Island for Further Plans
Canasta—Card Game Craze • Ice Cream Sandwiches
Sit Down, You're Rocking the Boat, & *My Destiny*—Songs

NOVEMBER
Nixon Is Elected to Congress from California
1st Jet Combat as US F-80 Downs Korean MIG-15
Lavender Hill Mob—Movie • *Call Me Madam*—B'way
Empire State Building Gets TV Tower, Making It 1,472 Feet Tall

DECEMBER
Diner's Club Brings US Credit Cards
Ralph Bunche Gets Nobel Peace Prize
Truman Declares National Emergency over Korea
Ma Perkins, Stella Dallas, & *Jack Armstrong All American Boy*—Radio

SONGS

I Can Dream Can't I?
Goodnight Irene
A Bushel and a Peck
The Thing
Tennessee Waltz

MOVIES

All About Eve
Born Yesterday
Sunset Boulevard
Asphalt Jungle
Father of the Bride

BOOKS

*Look Younger
Live Longer*
The Wall
Jubilee Trail
*Betty Crocker's
Picture Cook Book*
Kon Tiki

1951

JANUARY

North Koreans Attack and Recapture Seoul
Truman Budget $71.6 Billion, $41 Billion for Military
Air Force Atomic Tests Near Las Vegas
Are Felt as Far Away as San Francisco

FEBRUARY

Sugar Ray Robinson Beats Jake LaMotta
22nd Amendment Ratified by Nevada:
It Says No Person May Be President for More Than 2 Terms
US Population: 153 Million • S&H Green Stamps

MARCH

MacArthur Publicly Calls for Attacks on Red China
Dennis the Menace—Hank Ketchum—Cartoon
Gorgeous George—Wrestler • Lacoste Alligator Shirts
The Sea Around Us—Book • *How High the Moon*—Song

APRIL

Eisenhower Sets Up NATO Headquarters in Paris
MacArthur Tells Congressmen He Wants Victory
Truman Removes MacArthur from Command in Korea
and Puts Matt Ridgeway in Charge, Causing Public Outcry

MAY

WW II Veterans Benefits Extended to Korean GIs
In England, Guy Burgess and Donald MacLean Defect
to Russia for Whom They Have Been Spying
Mickey Mantle Joins Joe Dimaggio in Yankee Outfield

JUNE

Dean Martin and Jerry Lewis—*Colgate Comedy Hour*, &
Amos and Andy—TV • CBS Begins to Broadcast in Color
1st Commercial Computer Univac Goes on Sale
Military Service 2 Years Starting at 18½ Years Old

HEADLINES

The Korean War
Continues

Truman Removes
MacArthur

Britain and Egypt Clash
Over Suez Canal

1st Coast to Coast
Television Shows

USSR Explodes A-Bomb

1951

JULY

Indians Bob Feller Pitches 3rd No-Hit Game
Mississippi River Floods Cover 1 Million Acres and
Cause Over $1 Billion in Damage
Govenor Stevenson Calls Out Troops in Cicero, Illinois Race Riots

AUGUST

At UN Britain Asks Egypt to Lift Suez Blockade
St Louis Browns Manager Veeck Signs Midget to Bat
Because the Strike Zone Is So Small, He Gets Walks
Local Phone Calls Go from 5¢ to 10¢ in Some Places

SEPTEMBER

In San Francisco, 49 Nations Sign Final Peace
Treaty with Japan, US Maintains Troops There
1st Coast to Coast TV Networks—*Red Skelton, Studio One*
Heart Break Ridge Korea · *Because of You*—Song

OCTOBER

Bobby Thompson's Shot Heard Round the World,
3 Run Homer in 9th Brings the Giants the Pennant
The Lucy Show—TV · *A Place in the Sun*—Movie
Transcontinental Dial Telephones from New Jersey

NOVEMBER

New Jersey Turnpike Opens Philly to NYC
Studebaker 3 Window Business Coupe $1,643
Arthur Godfrey Finds Julius La Rosa on *Talent Scouts*
See It Now—Edward R Murrow—CBS—TV · Chevy Bel-Air $1,914

DECEMBER

Charles Oliphant Lawyer Resigns in IRS Scandal
1st Electricity from Nuclear Power in Idaho
Xmas Night, *Amal and the Night Visitors*—TV Opera
Flashbulbs for Cameras · *The Thing*—Movie

SONGS

*In the Cool Cool Cool
of the Evening*
Be My Love
Kisses Sweeter Than Wine
Come On-a My House

MOVIES

An American in Paris
*The Red Badge
of Courage*
A Streetcar Named Desire
*The Day the Earth
Stood Still*

BOOKS

From Here to Eternity
Return to Paradise
*JK Lasser's Your
Income Tax*
The Caine Mutiny
Catcher in the Rye

1952

JANUARY

Ike Says He Could Run for President
Truman Says IRS Should Be Civil Service, Not Political
Appointments as in Past • *Viva Zapata*—Movie
Today Show Airs Dave Garroway and J Fred Muggs

HEADLINES

King George Dies

Churchill Announces
England Has A-Bomb

President-Elect
Eisenhower Visits
Korea

Scrabble

Egyptian King Farouk
Goes into Exile

FEBRUARY

Truman Gets New Attorney General in Scandal
King Dead, Elizabeth's Coronation a Year Off
More UFOs in Skies and on Radar • *The African Queen*—Movie
The Illustrated Man—Book • Drive-In Movie Theaters

MARCH

Puerto Rico Becomes a Commonwealth
Batista Takes Over Cuba • *High Noon*—Movie
Truman Says He Is Not a Candidate
Joe McCarthy Squabbles with Other Senators

APRIL

Truman Orders Federal Troops into Steel Mills
Atomic Blast Carried Live on TV from Nevada
Matt Ridgeway Takes Ike's Place So He Can Run
Count Your Blessings Instead of Sheep—Song

MAY

Lillian Hellman Refuses to Answer HUAC Questions
Supreme Court Extends Freedom of Speech to Movies
Amy Vanderbilt's *Complete Book of Etiquette*
Living Coelacanth Caught off Madagascar

JUNE

I've Got a Secret—TV • Walt Kelly's *Pogo*
Supreme Court Finds Against Steel Mill Takeover
Ike Returns from Europe and Confers with Truman
McCarran Act Limits Immigration, Passed Over Veto

1952

JULY

SS *United States* Crosses Atlantic in 3 Days 10 Hrs
Ike and Adlai Stevenson Nominated
Cadillac 50 Years Old • The Transistor Radio from Sony
MacArthur Chairman of Board at Remington Rand

_____

_____

AUGUST

16,000 Escape from East Berlin • *Mad Magazine*
Parakeets, Panty Raids, Telephone Booth Stuffing—Fads
Howard Johnson Opens 351th Restaurant
Maureen Connolly, Bob Mathias, Hank Sauer—Sports

_____

_____

SEPTEMBER

Rocky Marciano Heavyweight Champ
Nixon Checkers Speech on TV • *A Man Called Peter*—Book
Jambalaya & *Your Cheatin' Heart*—Hank Williams—Songs
Pat and Mike—Movie • Pream—Cream Substitute

_____

_____

OCTOBER

8 NY Teachers Fired as Communists
1st Experimental H-Bomb • *Ozzie and Harriet*—TV
De Soto Power Steering, Power Brakes
Come Back Little Sheba—Shirley Booth, Burt Lancaster—Movie

_____

_____

NOVEMBER

I Saw Mommy Kissing Santa Claus—Song
Eisenhower Wins • Alexander Calder—Mobiles
Republicans Gain Control of Congress
George Meany Named Head of AF of L

_____

_____

DECEMBER

Auto Workers President Reuther Heads CIO
*Dinah Shore, Dragnet, Toast of the Town, Liberace,
Your Hit Parade,* & *Kay Kayser's Kollege of Musical
Knowledge with Ish Kabibble*—Popular TV

_____

_____

SONGS

Night Train
Blue Tango
Lullaby of Birdland
Do Not Forsake Me
Cry

MOVIES

The Quiet Man
*The Greatest Show
   on Earth*
Singing in the Rain
The Crimson Pirate

BOOKS

*The Power of
   Positive Thinking*
*The Old Man
   and the Sea*
East of Eden
My Cousin Rachel

43

1953

JANUARY

Ike Inaugurated · *Shane*—Alan Ladd—Movie
DMZ Set Up Between North and South Korea
15,000 Pizza Parlors, the Nation Loves It
San Francisco's Buena Vista Cafe Debuts Irish Coffee

HEADLINES

Korean War Armistice
Signed at Panmunjom

Queen Elizabeth
Crowned

Stalin Dies

Hillary Climbs
Mt Everest

Piltdown Man a Hoax

Crick and Watson Find
the Double Helix

Rosenbergs Executed

Corvette Shows Its
Fiberglass Body

FEBRUARY

Joe McCarthy Blasts Voice of America Broadcasts
US Chases Russian MIGs from Japan's Airspace
A Stillness at Appomattox—Book · *Ebb Tide*—Song
Sugar Smacks Cereal · IBM 701 Computer

MARCH

Ike Promises to Aid France in Vietnam
Dag Hammarskjöld Heads UN · *Pretend*—Song
US Thunderjet Shot Down Over Germany by 2 MIG-15s
but Pilot Escapes · *Dear John Letter*—Song

APRIL

Congress OKs Dept of Health, Education, and Welfare
Wayne Morse in Senate Fight Over Offshore Drilling
US Offers $50,000 and Asylum for Any North Korean
Defecting with Soviet MIG Jet · *TV Guide*

MAY

I Led Three Lives—TV · *Hi-Lili, Hi-Lo*—Song
Gentlemen Prefer Blondes—Movie · *Kismet*—Musical
Bwana Devil—3D Movie · *Battle Cry*—Book
Tea and Sympathy—Play · Native Dancer & Dark Star—Horses

JUNE

Film of Elizabeth's Coronation Rushed by Plane to US So
America Can Watch on TV · *Can Can*—Musical
Boston Red Sox Get 17 Runs in 1 Inning Against Detroit
US Air Force Plane Crashes in Tokyo, Kills 129

JULY

NY Subway Fares Increase from 10¢ to 15¢
Douglas Aircraft DC-7 Costs $1.5 Million
Batista Government Captures Fidel Castro
and Sentences Him to 15 Years in Prison

1953

SONGS

*Don't Let the Stars
Get in Your Eyes*
*How Much Is That
Doggie in the
Window?*
Vaya con Dios

AUGUST

CIA Gives Shah Upper Hand in Turmoil in Iran
214,000 Can Immigrate to US with New Refugee Relief Act
Olds Has Air Conditioning • *The Wild One*—Marlon Brando—Movie
US Forces Get Nike-Ajax Surface to Air Missiles

SEPTEMBER

Make Room for Daddy—TV • Bermuda Shorts
US Major General Dean Captured in Korea Released
In Geneva: France, Britain, and US Call on Russia to Meet
20th Century Fox's Movie *The Robe* Is in CinemaScope

MOVIES

From Here to Eternity
Stalag 17
Lili
Kiss Me Kate

OCTOBER

Earl Warren Becomes Chief Justice of Supreme Court
Federal Employees Using 5th Amendment Dismissed
Marshall Gets Nobel Prize for European Recovery
Mickey Mantle Hits Grand Slam Homer in World Series

NOVEMBER

*Captain Video, Life with Luigi, Marty,
Sky King, Kraft Theatre, US Steel Hour,
Our Miss Brooks, You Asked for It, Howdy Doody,
Beat the Clock,* & *Phillip Morris Playhouse*—Prime Time TV

BOOKS

*The Adventures
of Augie March*
The High and the Mighty
*How to Play Your
Best Golf*
A House Is Not a Home

DECEMBER

US Pulling 2 Divisions Out of Korea
1st *Playboy* Magazine Has Marilyn Monroe
Chuck Yeager Takes *X-1A* Rocket Plane to 1,650 MPH
Dow Jones Average Has Dropped from 294 to 255

1954

HEADLINES

The Postwar
Baby Boom Peaks

Nasser Seizes
Power in Egypt

Joe McCarthy Censured
by Senate

At Dien Bien Phu,
Ho Chi Minh
Defeats French

A Few US Advisers
Operate in Vietnam

Polio Vaccine

Roger Bannister Runs
Mile in Under
4 Minutes

JANUARY

Recession; Ike Proposes Cuts in Military Spending
Mamie Eisenhower Launches *Nautilus* Atomic Sub
Three Coins in the Fountain & *Sh-Boom*—Songs
Gal Gas 29¢ • Loaf Bread 17¢ • Dozen Eggs 60¢

FEBRUARY

Ike Reports 1st Hydrogen Bomb Test on Eniwetok
Unemployment Rate 5% • *This Ole House*—Song
Salk Polio Vaccine Given to Schoolchildren
Secretary of Commerce Bans Surplus Sales to Communists

MARCH

H-Bomb Blast in Pacific Bigger than Expected
and Radioactive Cloud Poisons Japanese Fishermen
Puerto Rican Nationalists Shoot Up Congress
Howard Hughes Buys RKO Pictures for $23 Million

APRIL

Ike Establishes Air Force Academy in Colorado
Supreme Court Rules TV May Run Quiz Shows
Domino Theory of Communist Takeover Leads US to Aid
Vietnam But Ike Doesn't Want "all-out war"

MAY

French Lose at Dien Bien Phu, Vietnam
Supreme Court: *Brown* vs *Board of Education, Topeka*
Congress OKs St Lawrence Seaway
Young at Heart, Cross Over the Bridge, & *Oh My Papa*—Hit Parade

JUNE

The Glenn Miller Story—Movie
Health Concerns about Cancer Sell More Filtertips
Strontium 90 in Milk Causes Worry about Fallout
Changes in Pledge of Allegiance Add "one nation under God"

1954

JULY

Dr Sam Shepard's Wife Murdered, He Will Be Accused
Ike Asks $101 Billion for Interstate Highways
Geneva Talks Divide Vietnam at 17th Parallel
Shake Rattle 'n Roll—Song • 1st Newport Jazz Festival

AUGUST

Communist Party Outlawed in the US
US Car Sales 7,169,908, Only 52,000 Imported
Ike Tells Red Chinese That to Attack Formosa They Will
"have to run over the 7th fleet"

SEPTEMBER

The Tonight Show with Steve Allen
Ike at Ground Breaking for 1st Atomic Reactor
Eddie Fisher Marries Debbie Reynolds • *Sabrina*—Movie
US and Canada Build Distant Early Warning Radar DEW

OCTOBER

Air Force OKs 1st Supersonic Bomber B-58
Ike OKs Training South Vietnamese Troops
Hurricanes Carol, Edna, and Hazel Hit East Coast
Willie Mays and Giants Win Series • *That's Amore*—Song

NOVEMBER

Iwo Jima Memorial Dedicated in Washington DC
Despite Ike's Appeal, Dems Win Control of Congress
Linus Pauling Wins Nobel Prize • *Hey There*—Song
Swanson TV Dinners • *Cha Cha Cha*—Dance Fad

DECEMBER

Rocket Sled Sets Land Speed Record 632 MPH
US Senate Censures Joe McCarthy • *Secret Love*—Song
Dow Jones Closes Above 404 • 4 Million Births in US
Disney TV Show Features Davy Crockett, 1 Million Hats Sold

SONGS

Earth Angel
Mr Sandman
Papa Love Mambo
Teach Me Tonight
The Happy Wanderer

MOVIES

On the Waterfront
Rear Window
The Country Girl
A Star Is Born

BOOKS

The Lord of the Rings
*Let's Eat Right
to Keep Fit*
I'll Cry Tomorrow
No Time for Sergeants

1955

US Pays $2 Million to Victims of Pacific Testing
Eisenhower Press Conference Televised
Crinolines, Poodle Skirts, Black Leather Jackets
Yellow Rose of Texas—Song • *Mister Roberts*—Movie

HEADLINES

Rock and Roll

Montgomery Alabama
Bus Boycott

Disneyland Opens
in California

James Dean Dies

North Korea
Brainwashed US
Servicemen

Dodgers Finally Beat
Yankees in Series

Ford Introduces
Thunderbird
for $2,944

FEBRUARY

The Millionaire—TV • *Autumn Leaves*—Song
Atomic Energy Commission Says Fallout from
A-Bomb Tests Equal 1 Chest X-ray for Every American
Over a Billion Comic Books Sold Yearly, Earning $100 Million

MARCH

50% Raise for Congress, Vice President, and Judges
Ike Says US Will Use A-Bomb in Case of War
Greasy Hair Popular • *Eloise*—Book
Eden Roc Hotel Opens in Miami • Special K Breakfast

APRIL

East of Eden—Movie • Churchill Resigns
Albert Einstein Dies • Civil War in Streets of Saigon
Readers Digest Won't Take Cigarette Ads
Damn Yankees—Musical • *Cattle Call*—Song

MAY

For World Peace Ike Will Meet "anytime, anyplace"
Billboard Has *Ballad of Davy Crockett* #1
Presbyterian Church OKs Women Ministers
Bus Stop—Play • *Silk Stockings*—Musical

JUNE

Soviets Shoot Down Navy Plane in Bering Straits
Draft Extended for 4 More Years • *Band of Angels*—Book
Ann Landers *Chicago Sun Times* • *Melody of Love*—Song
The Lady and the Tramp—Movie • Postal Employees Get 8% Raise

1955

JULY
Disneyland Opens in Anaheim, California
1st Summit in Geneva, US, USSR, Britain, and France
The Seven Year Itch—Tom Ewell and Marilyn Monroe—Movie
Lawrence Welk—TV • *Maybellene*—Song

AUGUST
Hurricane Diane Kills 179 and Cost Millions
$44 Billion Lost by Stock Market in 1 Day
Neiman Marcus Opens Branch in Houston
You'll Never Get Rich—Phil Silvers—TV

SEPTEMBER
65 Million Americans Are Working
Astronomers Say Part of Mars Is Turning Green
Ike Has Heart Attack, Hospitalized for 3 Weeks
Gunsmoke & *Highway Patrol*—TV • *The Tender Trap*—Movie

OCTOBER
The Honeymooners & *The Mickey Mouse Club*—New TV
Mickey Mantle, Yogi Bera, Pee Wee Reese,
Duke Snider, Roy Campanella, Gil Hodges,
Sandy Amoros, Elston Howard—Names in World Series

NOVEMBER
Richard Daley Elected Mayor of Chicago
General Motors 1st Corporation Earning $1 Billion a Year
Jasper Johns, Robert Motherwell, Willem de Kooning,
Larry Rivers, & Robert Rauschenberg—Modern Artists

DECEMBER
Rosa Parks Refuses to Give Up Her Bus Seat
Martin Luther King Leads Montgomery Bus Boycott
AFof L and CIO Merge, George Meany Is Leader
609 Auto Deaths Over Xmas Weekend, 35,586 for Year

SONGS
Rock Around the Clock
16 Tons
Unchained Melody
*Love Is a Many
  Splendored Thing*

MOVIES
Rebel Without a Cause
Blackboard Jungle
Bad Day at Black Rock
To Catch a Thief

BOOKS
Marjorie Morningstar
*The Guinness Book
  of World Records*
Bonjour Tristesse
Gift from the Sea
*Man in the Gray
  Flannel Suit*
Notes of a Native Son

1956

Miss Clairol Asks "Does She or Doesn't She?"
Rock and Roll Waltz—Song • *Friendly Persuasion*—Movie
Elvis Records *Heartbreak Hotel*, Soon to Be a Hit
President Asks for Soil Bank to Help Farmers

FEBRUARY

University of Alabama Enrolls 1st Black
Eisenhower Offers to Run for Second Term
Ike Vetoes Removal of Price Controls on Natural Gas
6 Million Cars and 1 Million Trucks Built this Year

HEADLINES

Suez Canal Crisis:
  Israel and England
  Take Suez Canal
  from Egypt

Russia Crushes
  Rebellions in
  Hungary and Poland

Peyton Place—A Book
  Shocks the Nation

Airliners Collide Over
  the Grand Canyon

MARCH

Minimum Wage Goes from 75¢ to $1 an Hour
156 Day Strike at Westinghouse Settled
"In 25 Words or Less" Contests Are Everywhere
1 of 8 Cars Is a Station Wagon • *Hot Digitty*—Song

APRIL

As the World Turns & *The Edge of Night*—TV Soaps
Labor Columnist Victor Riesel Blinded by Acid
6 Marine Recruits Drown at Parris Island Camp
Grace Kelly Marries Prince Rainier • *Lady Sings the Blues*—Billie Holiday

MAY

Pirates Dale Long Hits 8 Homers in 8 Games in a Row
B-52 Drops H-Bomb on Bikini Island Atoll
UN Inspection Team in Korea Fight Amongst Selves
The Bells Are Ringing—B'way • *Blue Suede Shoes*—Song

JUNE

Ike Hospitalized by Ileitis Attack Requires Surgery
Dr Salk Predicts Polio Will Be Gone in 3 Years
The Wayward Wind—Song • *Godzilla, King of the Monsters*—Movie
Comet • Imperial Margarine • Raid • *All Shook Up*—Elvis—Song

1956

JULY

End of *The Greatest Show on Earth* as a Tent Circus
Ocean Liner *Andrea Dorea* Hit by *Stockholm* and Sinks
Nasser Seizes Suez Canal • *My Prayer*—The Platters
"Drive a De Soto Before You Decide" • Studebaker Hawk

AUGUST

Democrats Nominate Stevenson in Chicago
"Don't Gamble with Poverty with the GOP"
GOP Nominates Ike and Nixon in San Francisco
"Don't Change the Team in the Middle of the Stream"

SEPTEMBER

Elvis Appears on Ed Sullivan, Shown Waist Up
Don't Be Cruel, Hound Dog, & *Love Me Tender*—Songs
My Fair Lady—Musical • Ankle Bracelets—Fashion
Ernie Kovacs Show—TV • *Around the World in Eighty Days*—Movie

OCTOBER

Don Larson Throws No-Hitter in World Series
Israel Invades Egypt • *The Last Hurrah*—Book
Olympics in Melbourne, Australia: Hungarians Win Water Polo
Match with Russians, Get Gold, Then Defect to America En Masse

NOVEMBER

Democrats Keep Control of Congress
Khrushchev Tells West: ". . .We will bury you"
3 US Scientists Share Nobel Prize for Transistor
Despite Health Problems, Ike Wins Re-election

DECEMBER

Nasser Has Sunk Ships in Suez Canal to Block It
UN Salvage Crews Start to Clear Them Away
To Tell the Truth—TV • Dow Jones Peaks at 521
Li'l Abner—Musical • *I Walk the Line*—Johnny Cash—Song

SONGS

Roll Over Beethoven
*Whatever Will Be
  Will Be*
The Great Pretender
Poor People of Paris

MOVIES

The Searchers
The Ten Commandments
Giant
*Invasion of the Body
  Snatchers*

BOOKS

Andersonville
The Nun's Story
Don't Go Near the Water
The Organization Man
*Arthritis and Common
  Sense*

1957

HEADLINES

Sputnik

US and USSR Build
  Intercontinental
  Ballistic Missiles

Civil Rights
  Confrontations in
  Little Rock, Arkansas

European Common
  Market

British Release
  Archbishop Makarios

West Side Story
  on B'way

JANUARY

Ike Asks Permission to Use Military in Middle East
State of Union Address Points to Growing Inflation
US Budget: $71 Billion • The Sack Dress—Fashion
Jailhouse Rock, Young Love, & Searchin'—Songs

FEBRUARY

US Trades Arms for Air Base in Saudi Arabia
Senate Investigates Corruption in Teamsters
You Send Me—Song • US Population Passes 170 Million
Asian Flu Kills Millions in US • *April Love*—Song

MARCH

Israeli Forces Turn Over Gaza Strip to UN Troops
Teamster Head Beck Uses 5th Amendment 80 Times
in Congressional Committee Hearing
Hoover Introduces Spin Dryer for Wash Days

APRIL

US Lifts Travel Ban on Egypt, Israel, and Mid-East
*People Are Funny, Lassie, Loretta Young Show,
Broken Arrow, Bob Cummings,
Sgt Preston of the Yukon,* & *Rin Tin Tin*—Prime Time TV

MAY

Sayonara—Movie • *Tammy*—Song
A Death in the Family & *The Wapshot Chronicle*—Books
Chiang Kai-shek Apologizes for US Embassy Attack
Senator John F Kennedy Wins Pulitzer Prize for His Book *Profiles in Courage*

JUNE

Khrushchev Hints at Possible Disarmament Talks
Supreme Court Nixes DuPont Buying General Motors
Mayflower Replica Sails Atlantic to Plymouth, Massachusetts
Silk Stockings—Cole Porter • Hurricane Audrey Hits Texas & Louisiana

1957

JULY

Scientists Have International Geophysical Year
Althea Gibson Wins Women's Tennis at Wimbledon
Funny Face—Movie • *Let Me Be Your Teddy Bear*—Elvis
Dear Abby Advice Column • Jack Parr Takes Over *The Tonight Show*

AUGUST

Calypso Music Craze Led by Harry Belafonte
Last Steam Locomotive, Atchison, Topeka, & Santa Fe
Eisenhower Proposes 2-Year Nuclear Test Ban
Senator Strom Thurmond Filibusters for 24 Hours

SEPTEMBER

Ike Signs 1st Civil Rights Bill in 87 Years
1st Underground Testing in Nevada
Riots in Little Rock Slow Desegregation
Have Gun Will Travel, Perry Mason, & *Wagon Train*—TV

OCTOBER

1st *Sputnik* • *Leave It to Beaver*—TV
American Bandstand on ABC Network Nationwide
Queen Elizabeth and Phillip Tour US and Canada
Head of Murder Incorporated Murdered in New York City

NOVEMBER

Appalachian Mafia Pow Wow Broken Up by G-Men
$64,000 Question, $64,000 Challenge, & *Twenty-One*
—TV Quiz Shows Fascinate the Nation
Eisenhower Suffers Mild Stroke • US Occupation Troops Leave Japan

DECEMBER

Teamsters Forced from AFL-CIO
Ike Is 1st President to Visit Paris Since Wilson
Shippingport Pennsylvania: 1st Full-sized Atomic Power Plant
On the Road—Jack Keroac—Book • *Chances Are*—Johnny Mathis—Song

SONGS

All the Way
Peggy Sue
Maria
Party Doll
Love Letters in the Sand
The Banana Boat Song

MOVIES

*The Bridge on the
   River Kwai*
The Three Faces of Eve
Twelve Angry Men
Written on the Wind
A Face in the Crowd

BOOKS

The Cat in the Hat
   —Dr Seuss
*Kids Say the Darndest
   Things*
*Please Don't Eat
   the Daisies*
The Hidden Persuaders
Atlas Shrugged

1958

JANUARY

9,000 Scientists from 43 Countries Ask UN's
Dag Hammarsköld to Halt Nuclear Tests
Gallup Poll Has Eleanor Roosevelt Most Admired Woman
1st US Satellite, *Explorer 1* • Cocoa Puffs—Breakfast

HEADLINES

US Gets into Space Race

Communist Chinese
Shell Offshore Islands

De Gaulle Becomes
Premier of France

Jets for Commercial
Aviation, Domestic
and International

Ike's Xmas Message
Broadcast from
Satellite in Space

FEBRUARY

BankAmericard and American Express Card in US
First Class Mail Increases from 3¢ to 4¢
Jeans $3.75 • Median Family Income $5,000 • Nathan's Dog 25¢
Gas 30¢ a Gallon • Hospital Room $28 a Day • Newspaper 5¢

MARCH

Atomic Sub Skate Crosses Atlantic in 8 Days
2nd US Satellite *Vanguard 1*, Proves Earth Not Round
Elvis Enters Army, Haircut • *Tom Dooley*—Song
Havana Hilton Opens • *Our Man in Havana*—Book

APRIL

Van Cliburn Wins Piano Competition in Moscow
US Begins Atomic Testing on Eniwetok in Pacific
New York Giants Move to San Francisco
Brooklyn Dodgers Move to Los Angeles

MAY

US and Canada Form North American Air Defense
Command (NORAD) • Congress Starts FAA
Nixon Jostled by Hostile Crowds in South America
I Want to Live—Movie • Sweet 'n Low

JUNE

US Helicopter Makes Emergency Landing in East Germany
Chevy Introduces Impala • Ford Introduces Edsel
Ike's Aide, Sherman Adams, Testifies in Congress
Pat Boone's White Buck Shoes • Hula Hoops

1958

JULY
Eisenhower Sends Marines to Lebanon
Red Cross Gets US Helicopter Crew Out of Germany
Ike Signs Space Bill, NASA Born · *Vertigo*—Movie
Catch a Falling Star & *At the Hop*—Songs

AUGUST
Sub *Nautilus* Makes Undersea Crossing of North Pole
Sherman Adams' Friend, Bernard Goldfine, Cited for
Contempt of Congress · *King Creole*—Movie
US Continues to Withhold Recognition of Red China

SEPTEMBER
Gracie Allen Retires · *Peter Gunn*—TV
1st *America's* Cup Since 1937, *Columbia* Sails for US
Rockin' Robin, Little Star, & *It's All in the Game*—Songs
Governor Faubus Closes Little Rock Schools, Classes Held on TV

OCTOBER
Red Chinese Say They Will Bombard Nationalist
Chinese Islands Only on Odd-Numbered Days
Regular Jet Service Starts, US to Europe
77 Sunset Strip—TV · *Volare*—Song · Folk Music

NOVEMBER
Democrats Gain 63 Seats in Congress
Bird Dog—Everly Bros—Song · *Father Knows Best*—TV
Get a Job—Song · Khrushchev Wants West Out of Berlin
Nelson Rockefeller , NY Governor · *Only in America*—Book

DECEMBER
Johnny Unitas Leads Colts Over Giants in NFL
Masters of Deceit—Book · John Birch Society Founded
To Know Him Is to Love Him—Song · *The Entertainer*—B'way
Buddy Holly Has 7 Top 40 Hits · 375 Daily Newspapers in US

SONGS
Fever—Peggy Lee
That'll Be the Day
Maybe Baby
The Chipmunk Song
Tequila

MOVIES
Touch of Evil
The Defiant Ones
Gigi
Thunder Road
The Big Country
Cat on a Hot Tin Roof—
Burl Ives

BOOKS
The Affluent Society
Ugly American
Anatomy of a Murder
Aku Aku

1959

JANUARY

The Batista Regime Falls and US Recognizes Castro
Alaska Becomes the 49th and Largest State
New York City Considers Becoming a State
Ford Falcon: Detroit's Answer to Smaller Foreign Cars

FEBRUARY

Integrated Virginia Schools Open Without Incident
Buddy Holly and The Big Bopper Die in Plane Crash
Carl Sandburg Addresses Congress on Lincoln's Birthday
Tornadoes Leave St Louis a Disaster Area

HEADLINES

Alaska and Hawaii
  Statehood

Castro Takes Cuba

St Lawrence Seaway
  Opens

NASA Chooses
  1st 7 Astronauts

Bolshoi Ballet Makes
  1st US Appearance

Chinese Take Tibet
  Forcing Dalai Lama
  to Flee

Nixon and Khrushchev
  in Kitchen Debate

MARCH

Pioneer Rocket Misses Moon, Orbits Sun
"Duck and Cover" A-Bomb Attack Drills
"Kookie Kookie Lend Me Your Comb"
Heartaches by the Number—Song • Volvo Puts Seat Belts in Cars

APRIL

Some Like It Hot—Movie • *The Miracle Worker*—Play
Oklahoma Repeals Prohibition
NASA Says We Will Have Man on Moon by 1969
Castro Tours New York, US, and Canada

MAY

Major General Ben Davis 1st Black to Hold That Rank
Olympic Committee Won't Recognize Formosa
NASA Sends Two Monkeys on Space Mission
Venus—Song • *Pillow Talk*—Movie • *Mr Blue*—Song

JUNE

Postmaster Bans Book *Lady Chatterley's Lover*
Ike and Queen Elizabeth Open St Lawrence Seaway
Johanson KOs Floyd Patterson in Yankee Stadium
He's Got the Whole World in His Hands—Song

1959

JULY
NY Governor Wants Compulsory Fallout Shelters
Federal Court Now Allows *Lady Chatterley's Lover*
Mamie Eisenhower Christens 1st Atomic Merchant Ship, *Savannah*
The Battle of New Orleans & *Lonely Boy*—Songs

AUGUST
Hawaii Becomes 50th and Smallest State
It Sends 2 Senators and 1 Representative to Congress
Making 100 in Senate and 437 in House
NASA Launch Sends Back Picture of Earth from Space

SEPTEMBER
What'd I Say—Ray Charles Hit • *Bonanza*—TV
Senate Raises Gas Tax 1¢ Per Gal to Pay for Interstates
United Council of Churches Says 64% Attend Church
Khrushchev Tours US But Can't Go to Disneyland

OCTOBER
Congress Will Override Ike's Veto 150 Times
The Twilight Zone—TV • Pele Scores 127 Soccer Goals
Fiorello—Musical • Dodge Push Button Shift in Dash
Ike Uses Taft Hartley to End Steel Strike

NOVEMBER
The *Triton* Becomes the Largest Atomic Sub Built
Disc Jockey Alan Freed Resigns in Payola Scandal
Charles Van Doren Admits Before Congress to Being Given
the Answers to TV Quiz Show *Twenty-One*

DECEMBER
Walter Wims Last Civil War Vet Dies, 117 Years Old
Ike returns from Tour of Europe, Asia, and Africa
$4,892 Buys Cadillac with Biggest Fins Ever
The American Football League Is Formed

SONGS

*Smoke Gets
  in Your Eyes*
Mack the Knife
Kansas City
16 Candles
A Teenager in Love

MOVIES

North by Northwest
Ben-Hur
Gidget
Sleeping Beauty
The Diary of Anne Frank

BOOKS

The Naked Lunch
Goodbye Columbus
*Dear and Glorious
  Physician*
The Elements of Style

57

1960

JANUARY

John F Kennedy Announces Presidential Candidacy
Ike Boasts of $200 Million Surplus in Budget and
the Most Prosperous Year in Our Nation's History
Nixon Says He's Running • *Exodus*—Movie

FEBRUARY

70,000 Students Sit-In in North Carolina
8th Winter Olympics in Squaw Valley
France Gets A-Bomb • Adolph Coors III Kidnapped
The Alamo—Movie • *Running Bear*—Song

HEADLINES

Adolph Eichmann
Captured

Khrushchev Bangs
His Shoe at UN

Sharpsville Massacre
in South Africa

U-2 Spy Plane

World Population:
3 Billion

US Population:
179.3 Million

OPEC Formed

Kennedy 35th President

MARCH

Supreme Court Makes Carter's Little Liver Pills Leave
Out the Word *Liver*, There Isn't Any in the Pills
Astro Turf Used in the Astrodome in Houston, Texas
Aluminum Cans for Soft Drinks

APRIL

US Launches *Tiros 1*, 1st Weather Satellite
JFK Wins Several Primaries and Says
"I don't think that my religion is anyone's business"
US GNP: $503 Billion, of which the Government Spends 27%

MAY

Carryl Chessman Dies in San Quentin Gas Chamber
Russia Shoots Down U2 Spy Plane and Gary Powers
1st Birth Control Pills • *Teen Angel*—Song
Israelis Capture Adolph Eichmann in Argentina

JUNE

The Rise and Fall of the Third Reich—Book
Floyd Patterson Wins Title Back from Ingmar Johanson
Itsie Bitsie Teenie Weenie Yellow Polka Dot Bikini—Song
Theater of the Absurd • *Camelot*—Musical

1960

JULY

Ike Cuts Cuban Sugar Imports to US by 95%
Khrushchev Threatens Missiles to Protect Cuba
An Evening with Mike Nichols and Elaine May—B'way
215 Million Frozen Dinners Sold in US Yearly

AUGUST

17th Olympics in Rome, Cassius Clay Boxing
Pentel Introduces the Felt Tip Pen
1st Communications Satellite Launched *Echo 1*
Bye Bye Birdie—B'way • *The Chapman Report*—Book

SEPTEMBER

Braves Warren Spahn Pitches No-Hitter
There Is 1 Car for Every 3 Americans
In His Last at Bat, Ted Williams Hits a Home Run
Atomic-Powered Aircraft Carrier *Enterprise* Launched

OCTOBER

4 Presidential Debates on National Television
Bulova Accutron 1st Electonic Watch • *Route 66*—TV
Elmer Gantry—Movie • *A Man for All Seasons*—Play
Georgia on My Mind, Stay, & *Cathy's Clown*—Songs

NOVEMBER

JFK Beats Nixon Narrowly • Campaign Slogans
"Mamie Start Packing, The Kennedys Are Coming"
"Kennedy Is the Remedy" • "Experience Counts Nixon-Lodge"
Hurricane Donna Hits East Coast

DECEMBER

Roger Maris, Joe Belino, Boston Celtics,
Philadelphia Eagles, Bobby Fischer, Ernie Banks
Rafer Johnson, Arnold Palmer—Names in Sports
2 Airliners Collide Over New York City, Killing 134

SONGS

El Paso
Chain Gang
Alley-Oop
*Save the Last Dance
   for Me*
*Are You Lonesome
   Tonight?*

MOVIES

The Apartment
Psycho
Butterfield 8
Inherit the Wind

BOOKS

Advise and Consent
To Kill a Mockingbird
Rabbit Run

1961

JANUARY

Kennedy "Ask not what your country can do for you, ask what you can do for your country . . ."
Ike Warns of " . . . military industrial complex"
US Rockets Chimp into Space • *Sing Along with Mitch*—TV

FEBRUARY

IBM Ball Typewriter • *The Executive Coloring Book*
Bouffant Hairdos • The Pillbox Hat • Coffee Mate
Sprite Soft Drink • Duncan Yo-yos • Total Cereal
Canned Dog Food • Kodachrome II • Jolly Green Giant

MARCH

JFK Creates Peace Corps and Alliance for Progress
Mattel Introduces Ken, a Boyfriend for Barbie Doll
JFK Introduces National Physical Fitness Program
Where the Boys Are—Spring Break Fort Lauderdale—Movie

APRIL

Russians Have 1st Man in Space, Yuri Gagarin
The Magnificent Seven—Movie • *Surfside Six*—TV
Warren Spahn Pitches 2nd No-Hitter • *Runaway*—Song
San Francisco Giants Willie Mays Has 4 Homers in 1 Game

MAY

Alan Shepard Goes into Space for US in *Freedom* 7
Minimum Wage $1.15 per Hour • *Mother-in-Law*—Song
Castro Wants to Trade Prisoners for 500 US Bulldozers
Newton Minow Calls TV " . . . a vast wasteland"

JUNE

*Wagon Train, Dobie Gillis, Hazel, The Perry Como Show,
Cheyenne,* Vince Edwards as *Dr Ben Casey, Rawhide,*
Richard Chamberlain as *Dr Kildare, The Flintstones,
Car 54 Where Are You?, The Twist* Introduced on *Ed Sullivan Show*—TV

HEADLINES

Cold War Heats Up

US Breaks Relations
with Cuba

1st Man in Space

Bay of Pigs Invasion

1st Plane Hijacked
to Cuba

Berlin Wall Goes Up

Dag Hammarsköld
Killed in Congo
Plane Crash

Russian Ballet Star
Nureyev Defects
to West

1961

JULY   *The Guns of Navarone*—Movie • *Travelin' Man*—Song
Catch 22—Book • FCC Allows Stereo FM Radio Broadcasts
JFK Has Eleanor Roosevelt Head Commission on Women
Buick Skylark $2,949 • *Stand by Me*—Ben E King—Song

AUGUST   *Two Rode Together* & *Splendor in the Grass*—Movies
Where Have All the Flowers Gone?—Song
Purlie Victorious—Play • *101 Dalmatians*—Disney Movie
Canton Ohio Chosen as Site for Football Hall of Fame

SEPTEMBER   Airplane Hijacking Made a Federal Offense
USSR Resumes Atmospheric Testing in Siberia
US Resumes Underground Testing in Nevada
The Bullwinkle Show—TV • *Runaround Sue*—Song

OCTOBER   JFK Says There Will Be Fallout Shelters for Everyone
Roger Maris Hits 61 Homers in Season, Breaks Record
Ernie Davis, Jerry Lucas, Rod Laver, Harmon Killebrew,
Gary Player, Minnestoa Gets Twins and Vikings—Sports

NOVEMBER   Rocket Plane *X*-15 Sets 4,093 MPH Record
Liz Taylor, Rock Hudson, Doris Day, John Wayne, Sandra Dee,
Cary Grant , Jerry Lewis, Tony Curtis, Elvis Presley—Top Box Office
The *Heidi* Game—A Children's Movie Bumps Jets and Raiders on TV

DECEMBER   2 US Helicopter Companies Arrive in Vietnam
They'll Shoot Back if Fired Upon, 1st American Killed
Michelob Beer • Burma Shave • *The Lion Sleeps Tonight,*
Please Mr Postman, Walk On By, & *Bristol Stomp*—Songs

SONGS

*Michael Row the Boat
Ashore*
*Will You Love
Me Tomorrow?*
Moon River
Big Bad John
Mama Said

MOVIES

The Hustler
Westside Story
Breakfast at Tiffanys
Raisin in the Sun
One Eyed Jacks

BOOKS

Franny and Zooey
Mila 18
Tropic of Capricorn
*The Making of
the President*
The Carpetbaggers

1962

JANUARY
Maximum Interest on Savings Accounts Raised to 4%
State Dept Says Cuba Base for MIGs and Soviet Troops
Stop the World I Want to Get Off—B'way
Nuclear Weapons Talks Fail after 39 Months in Geneva

FEBRUARY
US Swaps Col Rudolph Abel for Gary Powers U-2 Pilot
Jackie Kennedy Takes Us on TV Tour of White House
135 Million Watch John Glenn Orbit Earth on TV
The Errand Boy & *The Miracle Worker*—Movies

MARCH
Duke of Earl, Let Me In, & *Peppermint Twist*—Songs
Wilt Chamberlain Scores 100 Points in a Game
Billie Sol Estes Charged in Investor Swindle
Jack Parr Quits *The Tonight Show* • Esalen Institute

APRIL
JFK Forces Steel Companies to Take Back Price Raises
Century 21, World's Fair in Seattle Has Space Needle
US Resumes Testing at Christmas Island in Pacific
Johnny Angel—Song • *Mashed Potato*—Song and Dance

MAY
Happiness Is a Warm Puppy—Peanuts—Book
Scott Carpenter in *Mercury* Circles Earth 3 Times
Sex and the Single Girl—Helen Gurley Brown—Book
Stranger on the Shore—Acker Bilk Orchestra

JUNE
Supreme Court Rules Against School Prayer
JFK and Jackie Pay State Visit to Mexico
I Can't Stop Loving You—Ray Charles—Song
Stewardesses Demand the Right to Color Their Hair

HEADLINES

Cuban Missile Crisis

James Meredith at
  University of
  Mississippi

John Glenn 1st
  American to
  Orbit Earth

Thalidomide Babies

Marilyn Monroe Dead

1962

JULY

Roses Are Red, My Love & Palisades Park—Songs
The Gutenberg Galaxy—Marshall McLuhan—Book
The Man Who Shot Liberty Valance—Jimmy Stewart & John Wayne—Movie
Telstar Satellite Sends Live TV to Europe, 1st Picture an American Flag

AUGUST

Robbers Get Over $1 Million from Mail Van on Cape Cod
FDA's Kelsey Lauded for Stand Against Thalidomide
Loco-Motion & Breaking Up Is Hard to Do—Songs
Cesar Chavez Leads Farm Workers • Hatari!—Movie

SEPTEMBER

Intercollegiate Tiddlywinks • Diet Rite Cola
Beverly Hillbillies—TV • Sherry—The Four Seasons—Song
Bossa Nova & Watusi—Dances • My Three Sons—TV
A Funny Thing Happened on the Way to the Forum—B'way

OCTOBER

Johnny Carson Joins The Tonight Show—NBC TV
Kennedy Orders Blockade of Cuba Over Soviet Missiles
No More Cuban Cigars Because of Embargo
The Monster Mash, Ramblin' Rose, & Green Onions—Songs

NOVEMBER

Nixon Loses Bid for California Governorship
Russian Missiles Gone, Kennedy Ends Blockade of Cuba
Democrats Win in Off-Year Elections • Studebaker Avanti
Days of Wine and Roses—Movie • Beyond the Fringe—B'way

DECEMBER

Jumbo & What Ever Happened to Baby Jane?—Movies
Dow Jones 535 Down from 734 in 1961 • Telstar—Song
Maury Wills, Terry Baker, Don Drysdale, Willie McCovey,
Rod Laver, Jim Beatty, Hank Stram, Jim Taylor, Jerry Kramer—Sports

SONGS

Surfin' Safari
The Lonely Bull
He's a Rebel
Twisting the Night Away
Big Girls Don't Cry

MOVIES

Lawrence of Arabia
To Kill a Mockingbird
Mutiny on the Bounty
Lolita

BOOKS

Ship of Fools
Dearly Beloved
Youngblood Hawke
Seven Days in May
The Silent Spring

1963

JANUARY
5 Helicopters Shot Down in Vietnam, Death Toll 30
Da Vinci's *Mona Lisa* at National Gallery Washington
Donovan's Reef—Movie • *Password*—TV
LA Woman Tries to Kill Husband with Electric Toothbrush

_____

_____

FEBRUARY
Kennedy Proposes Domestic Peace Corps, VISTA
5¢ for 1st Class Mail • *Surfin' USA*—Beach Boys—Song
Spy Who Came in from the Cold—Book • *Hey Paula*—Song
Tanker *Sulphur Queen* Disappears in Bermuda Triangle

_____

_____

HEADLINES

Medger Evers Shot

In Britain
Great Train Robbery
   Nets $7 Million

Profumo Scandals

Civil Rights March
   in Washington

Washington—Kremlin
   Hotline Established

President Kennedy
   Dead in Dallas

MARCH
Supreme Court Says Defendants Entitled to Lawyers
Paris Introduces Knee-High White Boots
Barefoot in the Park—B'way • *PT 109*—Movie
Dr No—James Bond Movie • *He's So Fine*—Song

_____

_____

APRIL
Atomic Sub *Thresher* Sinks off Cape Cod, 129 Lost
Life Savers Are 50 Years old • *Cat's Cradle*—Book
I Will Follow Him & *Our Day Will Come*—Songs
Martin Luther King Arrested in Birmingham Demonstration

_____

_____

MAY
Alcatraz Prison in San Francisco Bay Closed
NASA Sends Gordon Cooper on 22 Orbit Mission
USSR Says It Will Not Pay Its Bills at the UN
Coke Introduces Tab • *Lillies of the Field*—Movie

_____

_____

JUNE
JFK at the Berlin Wall, "Ich bin ein Berliner"
The Birds, Son of Flubber, & *America America*—Movies
The Monkee and *The Slauson* Are the Latest Dances
Surf City—Song • Dr DeBakey Uses 1st Artificial Heart

_____

_____

1963

JULY

Puff the Magic Dragon, It's My Party, Memphis, Sukiyaki, Blue on Blue, So Much in Love, Fingertips Part 2, Wipe Out, Blowin' in the Wind, Tie Me Kangaroo Down Sport, & *Heat Wave*—Songs

AUGUST

Dr King at Lincoln Memorial," . . . I have a dream"
200,000 at Washington Civil Rights Demonstration
Hello Mudduh, Hello Fadduh—Alan Sherman—Song
Single Girls Janice Wylie and Roommate Murdered in NYC

SEPTEMBER

The Fugitive—TV • *If I Had a Hammer*—Song
Bomb Kills 4 Young Girls in Birmingham Church
College Students Smash Pianos as Part of Fad
Winston Churchill Made Honorary American

OCTOBER

5 Baseball Players Earn Over $100,000 While It Is the
First Time Factory Workers Average Over $100 a Week
Bob Cousy, Pete Rozelle, George Halas, Jim Brown,
Roger Staubach, Leo Nomellini, Whitey Ford—Sports

NOVEMBER

John Fitzgerald Kennedy Shot in Dallas

Lyndon Johnson Promises to Carry on Kennedy Ideals
102 Nations Represented at Funeral in Washington

DECEMBER

Guggenheim Museum in NYC Has Pop Art Show
Dominique—The Singing Nun & *Sugar Shack*—Music
Frank Sinatra Jr Kidnapped But Is Released Unharmed
Roche Labs Introduces Valium • *Deep Purple*—Song

SONGS

Go Away Little Girl
Walk Like a Man
My Boyfriend's Back
Blue Velvet
*Don't Think Twice
  It's Alright*

MOVIES

Hud
Tom Jones
Cleopatra
Irma La Duce
La Dolce Vita

BOOKS

The Group
The Feminine Mystique
Raise High the Roof Beam
The Reivers

65

1964

JANUARY

LBJ Calls for War on Poverty and $97 Billion Budget
East Germany Closes Border after 1 Million Have Left
White House Hootenanny with New Christy Minstrels
Etch-A-Sketch • Op Art • *Forget Him*—Bobby Rydell—Song

_____

_____

FEBRUARY

Cuba Cuts Off Water to US Base at Guantanamo
Beatles Appear on *Ed Sullivan Show* for $2,400
Cassius Clay Beats Liston, Becomes Muhammed Ali
Since I Fell for You—Song • Chevrolet Chevelle

_____

_____

HEADLINES

Gulf of Tonkin
  Resolution

US Begins Using
  Zip Codes for Mail

4 Civil Rights Workers
  Murdered in South

China Gets the Bomb

Race Riots in US Cities

Boston Strangler
  Captured

MARCH

1 in 3 Women Are Working • *The Pink Panther*—Movie
9.2 Earthquake and 220-Foot Tidal Waves Hit Alaska
Surfin' Bird, Louie Louie, & Hey Little Cobra—Songs
Kitty Genovese Killed in NYC, Her Cries for Help Ignored

_____

_____

APRIL

Beatles Have the Top 5 Songs on the Billboard Charts:
Can't Buy Me Love,   Twist and Shout,   She Loves You,
I Want to Hold Your Hand,   & Please Please Me
Lee Iaccoca and Ford Introduce the Mustang, It's a Hit!

_____

_____

MAY

Viva Las Vegas—Movie • *My Guy*—Song
Pop Tarts,   Maxim Coffee,   Synthetic Orange Juice
Senate Passes Civil Rights Bill
LBJ "time has come for . . . every American to get a decent break"

_____

_____

JUNE

Rudi Gernrich Offers Topless Bathing Suits
Jim Bunning Pitches Perfect Game for Phillies
Castro's Sister Defects from Cuba, She Had Helped CIA
People, A World Without Love, & I Get Around—Songs

_____

_____

_____

1964

JULY
Senator Barry Goldwater Wins GOP Nomination
Spacecraft *Ranger 7* Sends Back Pictures of Moon
Brain Drain Draws British Scientists to America
My Favorite Martian—TV • *My Boy Lollipop*—Song

AUGUST
British Music Invasion Begins After Beatle's Success
US Says Vietnamese Gunboats Attack Destroyer *Maddox*
California Becomes State with the Largest Population
Where Did Our Love Go? & *Under the Boardwalk*—Songs

SEPTEMBER
Warren Commission Report Says Oswald Acted Alone
House of the Rising Sun—Song • *Fail Safe*—Movie
Peyton Place & *The Man from U.N.C.L.E.*—TV Debuts
Petticoat Junction, I Dream of Jeannie, & *Get Smart*—Pop TV

OCTOBER
Martin Luther King Wins Nobel Peace Prize
Olympic Games in Tokyo, Seen Live on TV Via Satellite
565-Carat Star of India Sapphire Stolen from NY Museum
Baby Love, Dancing in the Street, & *Oh Pretty Woman*—Songs

NOVEMBER
Viet Cong Score Victory at Bien Hoa Air Base
Johnson Beats Goldwater, "All the Way with LBJ"
McDonald's Menu: Burger 15¢, Fries 12¢, Shake 20¢
Leader of the Pack—Song • *Zorba the Greek*—Movie

DECEMBER
Free Speech Movement on UC Berkeley Campus
Goldfinger—Movie • *Brillo Boxes*—Andy Warhol
Electric Carving Knives • Kelso, Horse of the Year
Jug Bands Feature Washboards, Tub Bases, and Kazoos

SONGS
Hello Dolly
Chapel of Love
Love Me Do
A Hard Day's Night
Do Wah Diddy Diddy

MOVIES
Dr Strangelove
Mary Poppins
Topkapi
The Disorderly Orderly

BOOKS
Candy
*The Man in His Own
    Write*—John Lennon
Armageddon

1965

JANUARY

LBJ Calls for Great Society Programs like Medicare
Rayburn Building Gives Congress New Offices
A Thousand Clowns—Movie • *The Shaggy Dog*—Dance
Love Potion Number Nine & *Help Me Rhonda*—Songs

FEBRUARY

Malcolm X Murdered in New York City
What the World Needs Now Is Love, Downtown, &
The Name Game—Songs • *Games People Play*—Book
US Starts Bombing North Vietnam • *Cactus Flower*—B'way

HEADLINES

1st American
  Space Walk

Watts Riots
  in Los Angeles

East Coast
  Power Blackout

Winston Churchill Dead

Joe Namath Gets
  $400,000 as Rookie

MARCH

LBJ Uses Alabama National Guard to Protect Marchers
Rights Worker Viola Liuzzo Shot During Selma March
US Forces Go on Offensive in Vietnam • *My Girl*—Song
The Great Race & *The Sound of Music*—Movies

APRIL

1st Indoor Baseball Game Played in Astrodome
Pontiac Introduces the GTO • All News Radio
King of the Road—Song • Carnation Instant Breakfast
Kodac Super 8 Home Movies • *Flipper*—TV • The Mod Look

MAY

Wackiest Ship in the Army, Shindig, Hullabaloo,
Run for Your Life, Combat, McHale's Navy,
Lost in Space, The Munsters, Gilligan's Island, F Troop,
Hogan's Heroes, & *Slattery's People*—TV

JUNE

51,000 Troops in Vietnam, Westmoreland Asks for
125,000 More, as They See Their 1st Full-Scale Combat
What's New Pussycat? & *That Man from Rio*—Movies
Back in My Arms Again—Song • Put a Tiger in Your Tank—Esso Ad

1965

JULY

(I Can't Get No) Satisfaction—Rolling Stones 1st Hit
Silver Dimes and Quarters Are Replaced by Alloys
LBJ Doubles the Draft • *A Thousand Days*—Book
The Loved One, Cat Ballou, & The Sandpiper—Movies

AUGUST

A Hard Day's Night—Movie • *Dune*—Sci-Fi Book
Mr Tambourine Man & *Turn, Turn, Turn*—The Byrds—Songs
Casey Stengel, 75, Retires from Managing NY Mets
I'm Henry VIII, I Am—Herman's Hermits—Song

SEPTEMBER

Sandy Koufax Pitches Perfect Game for the Dodgers
Castro Allows Discontented to Leave, Airlift Follows
I Spy & *Wild Wild West*—TV Debuts • *California Girls,*
Help!, Eve of Destruction, & *Hang On Sloopy*—Songs

OCTOBER

Congress OKs Anti-Pollution and Emission Standards
National Anti-Vietnam Movement Gains Momentum
Yesterday—Song • 5 Million Color TV Sets
NBC 95%, CBS 50%, ABC 40% Broadcasting in Color

NOVEMBER

51,000 Americans Killed by Cars This Year
Pentagon Says Over 1,000 Casualties in Vietnam
East Coast Power Blackout, 9 Months Later Baby Boom
Man of La Mancha—Musical • *Get Off of My Cloud*—Song

DECEMBER

US Stops Bombing North Vietnam for Christmas
Gemini 7 Up 14 Days Proves Moon Travel Possible
Chicago's Gale Sayers Scores 6 Touchdowns in 1 Game
The Dating Game—TV Debut • *The Ipcress File*—Movie

SONGS

You've Lost That Loving Feeling
I Got You Babe
This Diamond Ring
Stop! In the Name of Love

MOVIES

Doctor Zhivago
The Pawnbroker
Othello
The Sons of Katie Elder
8½—Fellini

BOOKS

The Source
Up the Down Staircase
Hotel
How to Be a Jewish Mother

1966

JANUARY

Cigarette Packages Must Carry Health Warnings
Paul Hornung and Packers Beat Cleveland Browns
We Can Work It Out—Song • *Gomer Pyle USMC* & *Batman*—TV
US Planes Collide Over Spain, Dropping Unexploded A-Bombs

FEBRUARY

US Announces It Will Be Selling Arms to Israel
Soviets Make Unmanned Soft Landing on the Moon
One Million Years BC, Thunderball, & *Harper*—Movies
Lightnin' Strikes & *These Boots Were Made for Walking*—Songs

HEADLINES

US Bombs Hanoi

Indira Gandhi
   Rules India

Truth-in-Packaging
   Laws

Daylight Savings
   Time Standardized

The Space Race

Time Magazine Man of
   the Year: Youth 25
   Years and Under

MARCH

LBJ Signs Cold War GI Bill of Rights for US Soldiers
Twister Game Introduced on *The Tonight Show*
General Motors Admits to Investigating Ralph Nader
Ballad of the Green Berets & *California Dreamin'*—Songs

APRIL

Time Magazine Cover Story Asks "Is God Dead?"
If I Were a Carpenter—Song • *Rush to Judgment*—Book
Dodge Charger—New Car   Oldsmobile Toronado: $5,125
New York's 1910 Pennsylvania Station Torn Down

MAY

Antiwar Rally at the Washington Monument
America's *Surveyor 1* Makes Soft Landing on Moon
Monday, Monday & *When a Man Loves a Woman*—Songs
Mark Twain Tonight—Hal Holbrook—B'way

JUNE

Gemini 9 Astronaut Walks in Space for 2 Hours
Supreme Court Hands Down Miranda Ruling
Paint It Black, Paperback Writer, Blonde on Blonde,
Born Free, Strangers in the Night, & *Revolver*—Music

1966

JULY
Mame—B'way • France Withdraws from NATO
John Lennon Compares Beatles' Popularity to Christ's
Wild Thing, Summer in the City, & I Am a Rock—Songs
Richard Speck Charged in Murder of 8 Student Nurses in Chicago

_____

_____

_____

AUGUST
Water Tower Sniper Terrorizes University of Texas
Lenny Bruce Dead in Los Angeles • *Cherish*—Song
Orbiter 1 Sends Pictures of Earth Back from Moon
Beatles Play Last Live Concert in San Francisco

_____

_____

_____

SEPTEMBER
Atlanta Hyatt Regency Opens in Peachtree Center
Reach Out, I'll Be There & *You Can't Hurry Love*—Songs
Star Trek & *The Monkees* on TV as Networks Go 100% Color
The Fortune Cookie—Movie • *Yellow Submarine*—Song and Movie

_____

_____

_____

OCTOBER
President Johnson Visits Troops in Vietnam
Mini Skirts • Paper Jewelry and Clothes • Pantsuits
Braves Move to Atlanta and Keep Hank Aaron
Bobby Hull, Frank Robinson, Roberto Clemente, Don Meredith—Sports

_____

_____

_____

NOVEMBER
Catholics Are Now Allowed to Eat Meat on Fridays
Ronald Reagan Elected Governor of California
Senator Edward Brooke Elected from Massachusetts
A Man for All Seasons—Movie • *96 Tears*—Song

_____

_____

_____

DECEMBER
The Flight of the Phoenix & *The Blue Max*—Movies
High Court Makes Georgia Legislature Seat Julian Bond
US Vietnam Troop Strength Up from 180,000 to 380,000
Total Traffic Deaths Are Now 3 Times Deaths in All US Wars

_____

_____

_____

SONGS

Sounds of Silence
Eleanor Rigby
Last Train to Clarksville
Sunshine Superman
Good Lovin'

MOVIES

*Who's Afraid of
  Virginia Woolfe?*
Seven Women
Alfie
Torn Curtain
Blow Up

BOOKS

Valley of the Dolls
The Adventurers
In Cold Blood
Tai-Pan

71

1967

JANUARY
Good Vibrations, I'm a Believer, & *Mellow Yellow*—Songs
Operation Cedar Falls in the Iron Triangle, Vietnam
Bart Starr Leads Packers to Win 1st Superbowl
Unisex Clothing   •   3D Tic Tac Toe   •   Super Tankers

FEBRUARY
25th Amendment Sets Presidential Line of Succession
Leonardo Da Vinci Painting Sells for $5,000,000
Turn On, Tune In, Drop Out   •   Cadillac El Dorado: $7,417
Ford Shelby Mustangs   •   *Grand Prix*—Movie   •   Camaro: $2,792

MARCH
A Fistful of Dollars—Clint Eastwood—Spaghetti Western
Georgie Girl, Bernadette, & *Ruby Tuesday*—Songs
Tanker *Torrey Canyon* Oil Spill   •   *The Dirty Dozen*—Movie
Thailand Base for US Bomb Runs into North Vietnam

APRIL
FDA to Study Effects of Smoking Dried Banana Peels
Grey Line Offers Tour of Haight-Ashbury and Hippies
Peace Marches in New York City   •   US Has 74 Nuclear Subs
Twiggy   •   Bra Burning   •   Frito Bandito   •   *The Naked Ape*—Book

MAY
Muhammed Ali Refuses to Enter Army, Stripped of Title
Let's Make a Deal—TV   •   *Groovin'*—Young Rascals—Song
Electric Circus, Electric Factory—Psychedelic Entertainment
AJ Foyt Wins Indy 500   •   Philadelphia 76ers Win NBA

JUNE
Jimi Hendrix Has Been Opening for The Monkees
He Becomes a Star at the Monterey Pop Festival
That Girl & *Family Affair*—TV   •   *Respect*—Aretha Franklin
Israel Attacks USS *Liberty* in International Waters

HEADLINES

3 Astronauts Die in Fire

1st Heart Transplant

6-Day War in
Middle East

Che Guevara Killed
in Bolivia

1st Superbowl Played
in Los Angeles

Summer of Love

1967

JULY

Sgt Peppers Lonely Hearts Club Band—Beatles Album
Mastercharge Cards • Expo 67 in Montreal, Canada
Fire on Carrier *Forrestal* Off Vietnam Kills 134 Servicemen
Surrealistic Pillow & *Between the Button*—Airplane & Stones Albums

AUGUST

Yippies Throw Dollar Bills Onto Stock Exchange Floor
Florida Drought Endangers Everglades Wildlife
Whiter Shade of Pale—Song • *Bonnie and Clyde,*
Doctor Dolittle, & *Guess Who's Coming to Dinner?*—Movies

SEPTEMBER

McNamara Asks $5 Billion for AntiBallistic Missiles
NASA's *Surveyor 5* Lands on Moon Testing Soil There
Death Toll in Vietnam Now 13,500 • Nehru Jackets
Never My Love—Song • *SRO*—Herb Alpert & The Tijuana Brass

OCTOBER

Thurgood Marshall Joins Supreme Court
NASA Venus Probe Passes near Planet Sending Pictures
The Virginian, Rat Patrol, The Flying Nun,
Green Acres, & *The Smothers Brothers Comedy Hour*—TV

NOVEMBER

1st Issue of *Rolling Stone Magazine* Hits the Stands
Point Blank—Movie • US Pop Passes 200 Million
Yacht Intrepid, Orlando Cepeda, Francis Chichester,
Carl Yastrzemski, Don January, John Newcombe—Sports

DECEMBER

The Beatles *Magical Mystery Tour* on TV
Almost 600,000 Troops Involved in Vietnam Now
Over 2,000 Planes and Helicopters Have Been Lost
Incense and Peppermints & *Day Dream Believer*—Songs

SONGS

Ode to Billy Joe
Pleasant Valley Sunday
Light My Fire
I Was Made to Love Her
Windy

MOVIES

The Heat of the Night
You Only Live Twice
Cool Hand Luke
The Graduate

BOOKS

The Chosen
Topaz
Our Crowd
The Confessions of
Nat Turner

1968

JANUARY

Deserting Soldiers Find Haven in Canada and Sweden
Rowan & Martin's *Laugh-In* on Monday Night TV
Chain of Fools & *I Second That Emotion*—Songs
LBJ Asks Americans for Economy to Not Travel Overseas

FEBRUARY

The Beatles Visit the Maharishi in India
Nixon Announces He Is Running for President
Peggy Fleming, Only US Gold in Winter Olympics
Planet of the Apes—Movie • *Judy in Disguise with Glasses*—Song

HEADLINES

TET Offensive

USS *Pueblo* Seized
  by North Korea

Johnson Says He
  Won't Run Again

Martin Luther King
  Assassinated

Robert F Kennedy
  Assassinated

Nixon Beats Humphrey

Russians Invade
  Czechoslovakia

MARCH

General Westmoreland Named Army Chief of Staff
Robert Kennedy Says He Is Running for President
Romeo & Juliet & *The Subject Was Roses*—Movies
McCarthy Wins 42% of Democratic Votes in New Hampshire

APRIL

Dr King's Assassination Sparks Riots Across US
In Vietnam US Troops Lift the Siege at Khesanh
Student Protests Close Columbia University
Listen to the Warm & *Lonesome Cities*—Rod McKuen—Books

MAY

1st Successful US Heart Transplant in Texas
Catfish Hunter Pitches Perfect Game for Oakland
Nuclear Submarine USS *Scorpion* Sinks in Atlantic
The Odd Couple—Movie • *Tighten Up*—Song • Blacklight Posters

JUNE

Woman Shoots But Does Not Kill Andy Warhol
Robert Kennedy Assassinated by Sirhan Sirhan in LA
MacArthur Park, *Mrs. Robinson*, & *Young Girl*—Songs
James Earl Ray Arrested in London for Dr King's Murder

JULY

Researchers Discover Bad Effects of MSG in Food
Cheap Thrills—Janis Joplin Album • *The Producers*—Movie
This Guy's in Love with You & *Grazin' in the Grass*—Songs
US, USSR, and 59 Nations Sign Nuclear Nonproliferation Treaty

AUGUST

Riots in Chicago as Democrats Nominate Humphrey
Stoned Soul Picnic—5th Dimension   *Hey Jude*—Beatles
Hello I Love You—Doors   *Jumpin' Jack Flash*—Stones
People Got to Be Free—Rascals   *Born to Be Wild*—Steppenwolf

SEPTEMBER

Hawaii 5-0, Mod Squad, & *60 Minutes*—New TV
Marshmallow Fluff on Fluffernutter Sandwiches
American Motors Javelin: $2,848   Ford Torino: $3,105
The Prisoner—TV • *Harper Valley PTA*—Jeanne C Riley—Song

OCTOBER

New Rating System for Movies: G, PG, R, and X
Barbarella, Oliver, Charly, & *Funny Girl*—Movies
Mexico City Olympic Games See Black-Power Salutes
LBJ Ends Bombing to Spur Vietnam Paris Peace Talks

NOVEMBER

Shirley Chisholm Becomes 1st Black Congresswoman
Hair Brings Counterculture and Nudity to B'way
More Bombs Dropped on Vietnam Than All of WW II
The Lion in Winter—Movie • *Love Child*—Supremes

DECEMBER

Apollo 8 Gives Viewers Xmas Eve TV Picture of Moon
Borman, Lovell, & Anders Orbit Moon 6 Times & Return
Don Schollander,   Bob Gibson,   Vince Lombardi—Sports
Light Shows Behind Rock Bands • Happenings • Multimedia

1968

SONGS

*Sittin' on the Dock
of the Bay*
Honey
Galveston
Sunshine of Your Love

MOVIES

2001—A Space Odyssey
Yellow Submarine
Rosemary's Baby
Bullitt

BOOKS

Couples
Myra Breckenridge
*The Teachings of
Don Juan*
The Population Bomb

1969

JANUARY

Joe Namath and Jets Surprise Colts in Superbowl III
USS *Enterprise* Fire, 25 Crewmen Dead, 85 Injured
Abraham, Martin, and John—Song · *Rachel, Rachel*—Movie
Nixon "We have found ourselves rich in goods but ragged in spirit"

HEADLINES

Astronauts Land
on the Moon

Chappaquiddick;
Woman Drowns in
Kennedy Car

Woodstock Festival

Altamont Rock Concert

My Lai Massacre
Discovery

Paris Peace Talks to
End Vietnam War

747s and Concordes

FEBRUARY

Lew Alcindor Plays Basketball at UCLA
Bob and Carol and Ted and Alice—Movie
Saturday Evening Post Magazine Quits After 148 Years
Everyday People, Crimson and Clover, & Worst That Could Happen—Songs

MARCH

Levi Strauss Markets Bell-bottom Jeans
Baseball Leagues Divide East and West
Apollo 9 Orbits Earth, Links Up with Lunar Module
Toy Makers Unveil Line of Black Dolls · *Proud Mary*—Song

APRIL

Yale, Princeton, Bowdoin, and Colgate Admit Women
Let the Sunshine in & *Time of the Season*—Songs
Peter Max Pop Art on Phone Books, Buses, and Subways
Now More Americans Have Died in Vietnam than Korea

MAY

Warren Burger Succeeds Earl Warren on Supreme Court
Apollo 10 Orbits the Moon 31 Times · *Room 222*—TV
Marcus Welby MD, Mayberry RFD, & *Governor & JJ*—TV
They Shoot Horses Don't They?—Movie · *Get Back*—Song

JUNE

Vietnamization: They'll Do More of Their Own Fighting
Cyclamates Banned for Causing Cancer in Mice
Travellers' St Christopher No Longer a Saint
Bad Moon Rising—Creedence Clearwater Revival—Song

1969

JULY

Troop Withdrawals Begin from Vietnam
Easy Rider—Movie • *The Peter Principle*—Book
Millions Watch on TV as Armstrong Steps Onto Moon
". . . one small step for man, one giant leap for mankind"

AUGUST

Woodstock Music Festival in Upstate New York:
A Celebration of Peace and Love by Thousands
Crosby, Stills, & Nash, Sly Stone, Richie Havens, The Who
Joe Cocker, Canned Heat, Country Joe, and Other Greats

SEPTEMBER

The Last of the Red Hot Lovers—Neil Simon
Oh Calcutta Shocks B'way • *A Boy Named Sue*—Song
The Love Bug—Movie • *Mr Rogers* & *The Forsyte Saga*—TV
Honky Tonk Women—Song • *Alice's Restaurant*—Movie

OCTOBER

New York's Miracle Mets Win the World Series
Nixon Says Vietnam War Will Be Over in 3 Years
Moratorium Day: Massive Antiwar Demonstrations
Altamont Festival: the End of Rock & Roll Innocence

NOVEMBER

Indians Seize Alcatraz Prison in San Francisco Bay
Nixon Appeals to Silent Majority in Attack on Press
Sesame Street: Big Bird, Kermit the Frog, the Muppets
2nd Americans to Walk on Moon: Conrad and Bean

DECEMBER

1st Draft Lottery Since WW II Held in New York City
Nixon Has Withdrawn 110,000 Vietnam Troops This Year
Down on the Corner & *Someday We'll Be Together*—Songs
Age of Aquarius: Communes in Vermont, Taos, Mill Valley

SONGS

*I Heard It Through
the Grapevine*
Aquarius
Sugar Sugar
Lay Lady Lay
Leaving on a Jet Plane
In the Ghetto

MOVIES

*Butch Cassidy and
The Sundance Kid*
Midnight Cowboy
True Grit
Chitty Chitty Bang Bang

BOOKS

Portnoy's Complaint
The Andromeda Strain
The Love Machine
*Linda Goodman's
Sun Signs*

1970

JANUARY
Gold Falls Below $35 an Ounce in London
United Mine Workers' Joseph Yablonski and Family Slain
The Greening of America—Book • *Medical Center*—TV
*M*A*S*H*—Movie • *Whole Lotta Love*—Led Zeppelin—Song

FEBRUARY
Linus Pauling Promotes the Virtues of Vitamin C
Up the Organization—Book • *Women in Love*—Movie
Raindrops Keep Fallin' on My Head—Song • *The FBI*—TV
Chicago 7 Trial: Abbie Hoffman, Tom Hayden, and Others

HEADLINES

Environmental
   Protection Agency

Ban on Cigarette
   Ads on TV

Beatles Break Up

Expo '70 in Osaka, Japan

Monday Night Football

Kent State Massacre

MARCH
Weather Underground Blows up NYC House
14 Army Officers Named in My Lai Massacre Coverup
NY Postal Workers Strike, 200,000 Follow Nationwide
Ford Maverick: $2,257   Dodge Challenger: $3,670

APRIL
Earth Day • American Motors Introduces the Gremlin
Apollo 13 Lands in Pacific After Troubled Moon Trip
Nixon Says 150,000 More Coming Home from Vietnam
US Invades Cambodia • *Let It Be*—Song • *Patton*—Movie

MAY
Nixon Calls Students Who Oppose Him "Bums"
National Guard Kills 4 Protestors at Kent State
NY Hard Hats Break Up Antiwar Protest, Injure 70
American Woman & *Spirit in the Sky*—Songs • Granny Glasses

JUNE
Senate Repeals Gulf of Tonkin Resolution
Platform Shoes • Peasant Dresses • Tie-Dyed Fabrics
Long and Winding Road & *The Love You Save*—Songs
Filmore Rock Theaters Close • Paris Peace Talks in 3rd Year

1970

JULY — Liberal Abortion Law Adopted by New York State
Cesar Chavez and Grape Growers End Farm Strike
Chet Huntley Signs Off NBC News, Last "Goodnight David"
Gary Trudeau's *Doonesbury* Syndicated in 30 Papers

AUGUST — Black Militants Kill Judge in San Rafael, California
Tora, Tora, Tora, Cotton Comes to Harlem, & *Joe*—Movies
Everything You Ever Wanted to Know About Sex...
...(But Were Afraid to Ask)—Book   •   *Close to You*—Song

SEPTEMBER — 59 Million TVs in America, 25 Million Are Color
60 Second Commercials Cost $65,000 on Prime Time
Ain't No Mountain High Enough—Diana Ross—Song
Jimi Hendrix Dead   •   *Five Easy Pieces*—Movie

OCTOBER — Boog Powell, Johnny Bench, Jim Plunkett, Billy Kidd
Curt Flood,   George Blanda,   Bobby Orr—Sports
Baltimore Orioles Beat Reds in World Series
Janis Joplin Dead   •   Solzhenitsyn Wins Nobel Prize

NOVEMBER — SALT Arms Control Talks Reopen in Geneva
Lovers and Other Strangers & *Ryan's Daughter*—Movies
I Think I Love You—The Partridge Family—Song
Natalia Makarova Defects to American Ballet Theater

DECEMBER — *Tears of a Clown* & *Fire and Rain*—Songs
American Deaths in Vietnam Average 25 per Week
Hello Dolly Closes on B'way After 2,844 Performances
448 Colleges Closed by Protests   •   Beethoven's 200th Birthday

SONGS

Bridge Over Troubled Water
Mama Told Me Not to Come
Your Song
Hello It's Me

MOVIES

Love Story
On Her Majesty's Secret Service
Airport
Little Big Man

BOOKS

The French Lieutenant's Woman
Islands in the Stream
QB VII
Ball Four
The Sensuous Woman

1971

JANUARY

Nixon Calls for Revenue Sharing with the States
Astronauts Spend 10 Hours Exploring Lunar Surface
Ms Magazine—Gloria Steinem • *Harold and Maude*—Movie
Lonely Days, Black Magic Woman & *My Sweet Lord*—Songs

FEBRUARY

Huge Earthquake Shakes Southern California
President Says He's Open to Dialogue with Peking
One Bad Apple & *Knock Three Times*—Songs
90 Dead, 500 Injured in Tornados in Southwest

MARCH

Bomb Explodes in Basement of US Capitol Building
Senate Cuts off Funds for Supersonic SST Plane
Charles Manson and "Family" Sentenced to Life
Me and Bobby McGee & *She's a Lady*—Songs

APRIL

Boy Scouts Eagle Division Admits Girls
New York State Allows Off-Track Betting
US Ping Pong Team Tours China • *For All We Know*—Song
Romper Room—TV • 200,000 in Washington Antiwar March

MAY

*Glen Campbell Goodtime Hour, Cannon, Ironsides,
Bewitched, Mission Impossible, Night Gallery,
Flip Wilson Show, Brady Bunch, Partridge Family,
Odd Couple,* & *Love American Style*—Prime Time TV

JUNE

Tricia Nixon Wed in White House Ceremony
Federal Marshalls Recapture Alcatraz from Indians
High Court Lets Newspapers Publish Pentagon Papers
Tapestry—Carole King & *Pearl*—Janis Joplin—Albums

HEADLINES

Voting Age
Lowered to 18

Vietnam War Spreads
to Cambodia and Laos

Pentagon Papers
Published

All in the Family
Goes on TV

DB Cooper Escapes

Red China
Given UN Seat

Hot Pants in Vogue

1971

JULY

US Post Office Becomes US Postal Service
Nixon Signs 26th Amendment: 18-year-olds May Vote
Astronauts Drive on Moon with Lunar Rover Vehicle
You've Got a Friend—James Taylor—Song • *Shaft*—Movie

AUGUST

Nixon Freezes Prices, Wages, and Rents for 90 Days
Causing Dow Jones to Jump 32 Points in 1 Day
Texas Instruments Offers 1st Pocket Calculator $149
How Can You Mend a Broken Heart?—Bee Gees—Song

SEPTEMBER

Kennedy Center for the Performing Arts Opens
Bloody Attica Prison Riot in Upper New York State
Chile Takes Over Copper Mines Owned by US Firms
Smiling Faces Sometimes—Song • *Columbo*—TV

OCTOBER

Walt Disney World Opens in Florida
UN Accepts Red China and Ousts Taiwan
1st World Series Night Game • *Jesus Christ Super Star*—B'way
Look Magazine Publishes Last Issue • *Maggie May*—Song

NOVEMBER

Mariner 9 Orbits Mars and Sends Back Pictures
DB Cooper Hijacks Plane, Parachutes with $200,000
Ecuador Seizes 42 US Ships, Claims 200 Mile Sea Limit
Gypsies, Tramps & Thieves, & Ain't No Sunshine—Songs

DECEMBER

Dollar at Record Low in Europe, Devalued by 8.5%
US Begins Large-Scale Bombing of North Vietnam
Bananas & *Dirty Harry*—Movies • *The Bell Jar*—Book
Alan Watts, Hugh Prather, Carlos Castaneda—Authors

SONGS

Joy to the World
Imagine
Brown Sugar
*Take Me Home
   Country Road*
Family Affair
Have You Seen Her?

MOVIES

The French Connection
Klute
Carnal Knowledge
A Clockwork Orange

BOOKS

Wheels
Passions of the Mind
The Day of the Jackal
The Betsy
*Bury My Heart
   at Wounded Knee*
Honor Thy Father

1972

JANUARY

Nixon Approves Space Shuttle Program
Nixon Announces He Will Seek Re-Election
The Foxfire Book • *An Old-Fashioned Love Song*
LA Lakers End 33-Game Winning Streak • *I'm OK, You're OK*—Book

FEBRUARY

California Supreme Court Rules Death Penalty Illegal
Nixon Arrives in Peking, Meets Mao
Jack Anderson Reveals ITT Gave Money to GOP
Without You, Sunshine, & *Never Been to Spain*—Songs

MARCH

North Vietnamese Launch Offensive Through DMZ
Heart of Gold & *A Horse with No Name*—Songs
Clifford Irving's *Howard Hughes Autobiography* Proves to be a Hoax
Pioneer Space Probe Goes 62 Million Miles, Passes Jupiter

APRIL

The Grateful Dead Tour Europe • *Trucking*—Song
Apollo 16 on Moon 3 Days, Brings Back Moon Rocks
US Starts to Bomb Hanoi and Haiphong Again
Polaroid SX-70 System Revealed • *Puppy Love*—Song

MAY

Nixon Orders Mining of North Vietnam's Ports
Governor George Wallace of Alabama Shot
Play It Again Sam & *What's Up Doc?*—Movies
Nixon 1st US President to Visit Moscow • *I'll Take You There*—Song

JUNE

Angela Davis Acquitted of Murder and Kidnapping
5 Arrested Breaking into Democratic Headquarters
Supreme Court Finds Death Penalty Cruel and Unusual
Sylvia's Mother—Dr Hook—Song • *Fritz the Cat*—Movie

HEADLINES

Mark Spitz Wins
7 Gold at Olympics

Israeli Athletes
Murdered

Nixon Visits Peking
and Moscow

Watergate Break-in

George Wallace Shot

Nixon Beats McGovern

JULY

McGovern and Eagleton Chosen by Democrats
Nixon Picks Spiro Agnew as Running Mate
Lean On Me, Song Sung Blue, & *Candy Man*—Songs
Sadat Says He'll Boot Out Russians for Not Selling Egypt Arms

---

AUGUST

Eagleton's Past Mental History Forces Him Out of VP Race
End of US Ground Combat Troops Fighting in Vietnam
Nixon Claims No White House Connection to Watergate
Brandy You're a Fine Girl—Song • *Deliverance*—Movie

SEPTEMBER

5 Watergate Burglars Indicted • *M*A*S*H*—TV
1st Time Since 1965 No Americans Die in Vietnam
Bobby Fischer Beats Boris Spasky, 1st US Chess Champ
Black and White & *Baby Don't Get Hooked on Me*—Songs

OCTOBER

White House: Gromyko and Nixon Sign SALT Treaty
Kissinger Announces Vietnam Peace Weeks Away
753 US Papers Support Nixon, 56 Back McGovern
Kung Fu—TV • *My Ding-a-Ling*—Chuck Berry—Song

NOVEMBER

Nixon Crushes McGovern, Worst Defeat Since 1936
Home Box Office Begins Broadcasting—Cable TV
Nights in White Satin & *I Can See Clearly Now*—Songs
Lady Sings the Blues, Summer of '42, & *Superfly*—Movies

DECEMBER

Nixon Orders New Bombing of North Vietnam
The Best and the Brightest & *The Boys of Summer*—Books
National Ban on DDT Begins • *I Am Woman*—Song
The Poseidon Adventure, Sounder, & *Straw Dogs*—Movies

1972

SONGS

American Pie
Brand New Key
Let's Stay Together
*Me and Julio Down
  by the Schoolyard*

MOVIES

The Godfather
Cabaret
*And Now for Something
  Completely Different*

BOOKS

*Jonathan Livingston
  Seagull*
The Winds of War
Semi-Tough
The Word
Open Marriage

1973

JANUARY

Airline Passengers Will Be Screened to Foil Hijackers
Nixon Wants to Limit Government Role in Daily Life
Roe vs *Wade*, Supreme Court Rules on Abortion Laws
Miami Ends Undefeated Season Winning Superbowl

FEBRUARY

Prisoner of War Exchange in Vietnam Frees 142 Men
We Are Consuming More Energy Than We Produce
American Indians Seize Wounded Knee, North Dakota
Killing Me Softly with His Song & *Crocodile Rock*—Songs

HEADLINES

Vietnam Cease Fire
Troop Pull Out
Peace!

Watergate Simmers
as Nixon Won't
Give Up Tapes

Gerald Ford Becomes
Vice President

Gas Shortage

Kohoutek Comet

Free Agents in Baseball

MARCH

Ervin Committee Suspects John Mitchell in Coverup
Marlon Brando Refuses Oscar for Role in *The Godfather*
Last American Troops Leave South Vietnam
Martha Mitchell Calls *NY Times* Reporter about Watergate

APRIL

Dean, Ehrlichman, Haldeman, Stans, Kleindienst, Cox,
Richardson, Gray, Liddy, & McCord—Watergate Cast
Nixon on TV Explains to Country About Watergate
Tie a Yellow Ribbon Round the Old Oak Tree—Song

MAY

Senate Committee Begins Watergate Hearings on TV
Tom Bradley Becomes Mayor of Los Angeles
You Are the Sunshine of My Life—Stevie Wonder—Song
NY Knicks Win NBA • Secretariat Wins Triple Crown

JUNE

Court Says "Community Standards" Define Pornography
Sonny & Cher Comedy Hour, *The Streets of San Francisco*,
The Waltons, & *An American Family: The Louds*—TV
Blume in Love & *Day for Night*—Movies • *My Love*—Wings—Song

JULY

Save the Tiger—Movie • *Gravity's Rainbow*—Book
Pentagon Didn't Tell Congress of Bombing Cambodia
1 Million Gather at Watkins Glen Rock Concert
Skylab Astronauts Embark on 59-Day Space Mission

AUGUST

Nolan Ryan Strikes Out 19 in 1 Day, 383 in Season
Sears Tower, Chicago & World Trade Center, New York
Vodka Outsells Whiskey for 1st Time
The Joy of Sex—Book • *Brother Louie* & *Live and Let Die*—Songs

SEPTEMBER

Henry Kissinger Sworn in as Secretary of State
Billie Jean King Gives Bobby Riggs Tennis Lesson
Bar Code Labels on Store Products • Mountain Bikes
Push-in Tabs on Cans Stop Litter • *Delta Dawn*—Song

OCTOBER

Watergate "Saturday Night Massacre," More Resign
Nixon Turns Over Tapes with 18-Minute Gap
Nobel Peace Prize, Kissinger and Le Duc Tho for Vietnam
OPEC Created and Bans Oil Exports to U S because of Israel

NOVEMBER

Leon Jaworski New Watergate Special Prosecutor
5 Big Corporations Admit Illegal Contributions to GOP
Angie, Ramblin' Man, & *Midnight Train to Georgia*—Songs
14 States Rewrite Death Penalty Laws • *Paper Chase*—Movie

DECEMBER

American League Allows Designated Hitter
Endangered Species Act • *Fear of Flying*—Book
Jackie Stewart, Jim Palmer, Tom Seaver, Charlie Finley
OJ Simpson, Phil Esposito, Ken Holtzman, Coach Madden—Sports

1973

SONGS

Bad Bad Leroy Brown
You're So Vain
Dueling Banjos
We're an American Band

MOVIES

The Way We Were
American Graffiti
Kung Fu Movies
*The Rocky Horror
   Picture Show*

BOOKS

Once Is Not Enough
*Dr Atkin's
   Diet Revolution*
*How to Be Your Own
   Best Friend*
Alistair Cooke's America
Sybil

1974

HEADLINES

Nixon Resigns

55 MPH Speed Limit

Patty Hearst Kidnapped

Pong Popularizes
Electronic Games

Hank Aaron Tops
Babe Ruth with
715 Home Runs

JANUARY

Major Oil Companies Earn Big Bucks Despite Gas Crisis
UCLA Loses to Notre Dame after 88 Basketball Wins
Nixon Pledges He Will Not Resign • *The Joker*—Song
Chico and the Man, Police Woman, Rhoda, & *Good Times*—TV

FEBRUARY

Patty Hearst Kidnapped by the SLA, Held for Ransom
You're Sixteen, Show and Tell, & *Jungle Boogie*—Songs
USSR Deports Novelist Alexander Solzhenitsyn
Nixon Says He Can't Be Impeached Without Evidence

MARCH

7 White House Staff Indicted for Watergate Coverup
Nixon Denies He Approved Watergate "Hush Money"
Streaking—Fad • *Working*—Studs Terkel—Book
Dark Lady, Seasons in the Sun & *Sunshine on My Shoulders*—Songs

APRIL

President Announces He Will Pay His Back Taxes
Bennie and the Jets & *Mockingbird*—Songs
CB Radios • Earth Shoes • Thongs • String Bikinis
ATC Motorbikes • Phone Phreaks • *Kojak*—TV

MAY

Senate Rejects Nixon Plea for More Vietnam Money
Judiciary Committee Opens Impeachment Hearings
FBI Says Patty Hearst Is "Armed and Dangerous"
Dancing Machine, The Streak, & *Sundown*—Songs

JUNE

High Court Rules "Equal Work-Equal Pay" for Women
Nixon Tours Mid-East, Visits USSR for Summit Talks
Mother of Martin Luther King Murdered in Atlanta
The Me Generation • *Lenny*—Movie • *Band on the Run*—Song

1974

JULY CBS Airs 1st *Bicentennial Minutes* • *Amarcord*—Movie
Supreme Court Rules Nixon Must Turn Over All Tapes
House Votes 3 Articles of Impeachment Against Nixon
Annie's Song & *Rikki Don't Lose That Number*—Songs

AUGUST Nixon Admits and then Resigns
Gerald Ford Sworn in as President • *I Shot the Sheriff*—Song
Ford Chooses Nelson Rockefeller as New Vice President
The Night Chicago Died & *Please Come to Boston*—Songs

SEPTEMBER *Harry and Tonto* & *Blazing Saddles*—Movies
Evel Knievel Attempts Snake River Jump
Carol Burnett, Mary Tyler Moore, & Bob Newhart—TV Shows
Ford Unconditionally Pardons Nixon • *Little House on the Prairie*—TV

OCTOBER Ali-Forman Fight in Zaire, Miami Dolphins
Oakland As Beat LA Dodgers in World Series, Steve Garvey,
Larry Csonka, Jimmy Connors, Football Overtime in Ties
Fran Tarkenton, Mike Marshall, Archie Griffin—Sports

NOVEMBER *I Honestly Love You*—Olivia Newton-John
Jazzman—Carole King • *Tin Man*—America
I Can Help—Billy Swan • *The Bitch Is Back*—Elton John
Nothing From Nothing—Billy Preston—Songs

DECEMBER *Kung Fu Fighting* & *Cat's in the Cradle*—Songs
All the President's Men—Woodward and Bernstein—Book
CIA Said to Have Conducted Illegal Domestic Spying
Towering Inferno & *Murder on the Orient Express*—Movies

SONGS

The Way We Were
*I Have to Say I Love You
in a Song*
Love's Theme
Hooked on a Feeling

MOVIES

The Sting
The Godfather, Part II
Chinatown
*Alice Doesn't Live
Here Anymore*

BOOKS

Watership Down
The Total Woman
*All Things Bright
and Beautiful*
*Tinker Tailor
Soldier Spy*
*Zen and the Art of
Motorcycle
Maintenance*

1975

JANUARY

Kissinger Hints US Action if Arabs Withhold Oil
High Court Says States Can't Refuse Women Jury Duty
Lucy in the Sky with Diamonds—Elton John,
Mandy—Barry Manilow, & *Fire*—Ohio Players—Music

FEBRUARY

The Mariana Islands Become a US Commonwealth
Judge John Sirica Sentences Watergate Conspirators
Hoover's Secret Files on Many Politicians Uncovered
Pick Up the Pieces—Song • *The Great Waldo Pepper*—Movie

HEADLINES

Saigon Falls
  to North Vietnam

Francisco Franco Dead

Patty Hearst Arrested

Jimmy Hoffa Disappears

New York Money Crisis

World Population
  Exceeds 4 Billion

MARCH

Work Begins on the Alaskan Pipeline • *Ragtime*—Book
Thailand Will Seek Withdrawal of US Forces
Best of My Love, Wolf Creek Pass, & *You're No Good*—Songs
UCLA Wins 10th NCAA Title, Coach Wooden Will Retire

APRIL

Ford Orders Withdrawal of Americans from Vietnam
  and Says Vietnam Not a Sign of American Weakness
You're So Beautiful—Joe Cocker—Song • *Rollerball*—Movie
Trash Compactors • Conrail Consolidates US Railroads

MAY

The Sunshine Boys & *Nashville*—Movies • *Baretta*—TV
New: Buick Skylark, $4,160 • *Helter Skelter*—Book
Land Sea and Air Forces Rescue USS *Mayaguez*
Congress Gives $405 Million to Vietnamese Refugees

JUNE

2 FBI Agents Shot on Sioux Pine Ridge Reservation
Ford Extends Unemployment Benefits to 65 Weeks
Supreme Court Says Defendants May Conduct Own Defense
Thank God I'm a Country Boy—John Denver—Song

1975

JULY

Congress Restores Full Citizenship to Robert E Lee
Apollo-Soyuz Space Link Joins US and Russians
Gerald Ford Announces His Presidential Candidacy for 1976
Jimmy Hoffa Missing in Detroit   •   *The Hustle*—Song

_____

_____

AUGUST

US Vetoes Entry of North and South Vietnam to UN
AFL-CIO Unions Refuse to Load Grain Bound for USSR
Ohio Governor and National Guard Innocent, Kent State Deaths
One of These Nights, Jive Talkin, & *Get Down Tonight*—Songs

_____

_____

SEPTEMBER

Patty Hearst Arrested   •   *Rhinestone Cowboy*—Song
Rising Malpractice Insurance Costs Hurting Doctors
Welcome Back Kotter—TV   •   *How Sweet It Is*—Song
Attempts on Ford's Life by 2 Women in California

_____

_____

OCTOBER

US-USSR Grain Deal for 6-8 Million Tons Yearly
Muhammed Ali Wins "Thrilla in Manilla"   •   *Benji*—Movie
Saturday Night Live—TV   •   *Island Girl* & *Lying Eyes*—Songs
BIC Disposable Razors   •   Pet Rocks   •   Waterbeds   •   Mood Rings

_____

_____

NOVEMBER

TVs Outnumber Bathtubs in the United States
President Says He Will Help NYC Avoid Default
Ford Makes George Bush New Director of the CIA
Six Million Dollar Man, Phyllis, & *Starsky & Hutch*—TV

_____

_____

DECEMBER

President Ford Visits China and Confers with Mao
Fred Lynn, Joe Morgan, Philadelphia Flyers—Sports
Palestinian Terrorists Hold OPEC Meeting Hostage
Let's Do It Again & *That's the Way I Like It*—Songs

_____

_____

_____

SONGS

Fame
Laughter in the Rain
Have You Ever Been Mellow?
Black Water
Philadelphia Freedom

MOVIES

Jaws
One Flew Over the Cuckoo's Nest
Dog Day Afternoon
Barry Lyndon
Tommy

BOOKS

The Choirboys
Winning Through Intimidation
Sylvia Porter's Money Book

1976

HEADLINES

US Bicentennial
   America Celebrates
   200th Birthday

Raid on Entebbe,
   Idi Amin Dictator

Nadia Comaneci Wows
   Montreal Olympic
   Games

Legionnaires' Disease

Swine Flu

JANUARY

Congress Passes $45 Billion in Social Programs
Scandal Shows CIA Gave Millions to Italian Politicians
Lynn Swann, Terry Bradshaw, and Steelers Win Superbowl
I Write the Songs—Barry Manilow & *Convoy*—CW McCall—Songs

FEBRUARY

Ford Beats Reagan in New Hampshire Primary
50 Ways to Leave Your Lover & *Mahogony Theme*—Songs
Famous Amos • Canon AE1 Camera • Christo's *Curtain*
Dorothy Hamill Haircuts • The Fonz • Reggae • Video Games

MARCH

Egypt's Sadat Moves His Country to Closer US Ties
2 Explosions in Kentucky Coal Mine, Kill 26
The Bad News Bears, Silent Movie, & *The Omen*—Movies
Love Machine, All by My Self, & *Take It to the Limit*—Songs

APRIL

Disco Lady—Song: 1st 45 Record to Go Platinum
Executive Suite, Adams Chronicles, Madame Bovary,
Rich Man Poor Man, & *Captains and Kings*—TV Miniseries
Philly's Mike Schmidt Blasts 4 Homers in 1 Game

MAY

IRS Reports 5 Millionaires Paid No Income Taxes
Supreme Court: Pharmacies Can Advertise Drug Prices
US and USSR Sign Treaty Limiting Underground Testing
Maude—TV • *Silly Love Songs*—Wings • *Taxi Driver*—Movie

JUNE

US Navy Evacuates Americans from Beirut
Ford Authorizes $6 Billion in Foreign Military Aid
Salt II Talks in Geneva • *Welcome Back*—John Sebastian—Song
US Ambassador and Aide Kidnapped and Killed in Lebanon

1976

JULY
Supreme Court Rules New Death Penalty Constitutional
Songs in the Key of Life & *Black and Blue*—Albums
School Bus with 26 Kids Hijacked in Chowchilla, California
Fireworks and Tall Ships in NY's Hudson River Celebrate 200th 4th of July

AUGUST
Flash Flood in Colorado River Canyon Kills 139
Shah of Iran Asks Additional $10 Billion in Arms
Ford Nominated at GOP Convention over Reagan
California Suite—Play • *Shake Your Booty*—Song

SEPTEMBER
Space Shuttle *Enterprise* Unveiled by NASA
Congressman Resigns for Having Mistress on Payroll
Charlie's Angels—TV • *Play That Funky Music*—Song
Chile's Ambassador Killed By Car Bomb in Washington

OCTOBER
Ford Slogan: "Betty's Husband for President"
Thousands Get Swine Flu Shots, Until 51 Are Paralyzed
US Sweeps Nobel Prizes; Saul Bellow Wins Literature
Frampton Comes Alive—Album • *The Bionic Woman*—TV

NOVEMBER
The Band Performs *The Last Waltz* in San Francisco
Carter Slogan: "I Work for Peanuts"
ERA Slogan: "A Woman's Place Is in the House and the Senate"
Carter Beats Ford • *Disco Duck* & *Rock'n Me*—Songs

DECEMBER
Bruce Jenner, Chris Everett, Cincinnati Reds—Sports
Thomas "Tip" O'Neill Becomes Speaker of the House
The Shootist & *King Kong*—Movies • *Muskrat Love*—Song
Rhodes Scholarships Open to Women • *Carrie*—Movie

SONGS

*Don't Go Breaking
My Heart*
Oh What a Night
Love Rollercoaster
Afternoon Delight

MOVIES

Rocky
Network
All the President's Men
Bound for Glory

BOOKS

Blind Ambition
*Roots: The Saga of an
American Family*
Hite Report
The Crash of '79

1977

JANUARY

Much of the Country Watches *Roots* Mini Series on TV
Gary Gilmore Dead in Utah, 1st Execution Since 1967
Carter Pardons Vietnam Draft Dodgers • *Lou Grant*—TV
75 Million Watch Oakland Raiders Win Superbowl

FEBRUARY

President Carter Cuts Foreign Aid to Countries
Who Are Accused of Civil Rights Violations
Fluorocarbons Banned in Spray Cans, They Hurt Ozone
New Kid in Town, Car Wash, Torn Between Two Lovers, & *I Wish*—Songs

HEADLINES

Elvis Dies

Son of Sam Caught

Star Wars Mega Movie

Canary Island Jumbo Jet
Disaster, 563 Die

Bert Lance Resignation
Mars Carter's Image

Disco Music

MARCH

Question and Answer Radio Show from White House
Carter Ends Travel Restrictions to Communist Nations
Evergreen, Rich Girl, & *Dancing Queen*—Songs
Congress Passes Stricter Ethics Code for Its Own Members

APRIL

Supreme Court Rules Teachers Can Spank Students
Don't Give Up on Us—Song • *Slapshot*—Movie
600 Exchanges Have 911 Emergency Phone Numbers
Switch, Rockford Files, Quincy, & *Grizzly Adams*—TV

MAY

1,414 Arrested in New Hampshire Nuclear Protest
Janet Guthrie 1st Woman in the Indy 500 Race
Carter Moves to Save the Social Security System
Hotel California—Eagles—Song—Album

JUNE

US and Cuba Resume Diplomatic Relations
Seattle Slew Wins Triple Crown—By the End of the
Month Jockey Steve Cauthen Has Won 525 Races
US Plans Neutron Bomb • *I'm Your Boogie Man*—Song

1977

JULY

Storm Triggers Another Huge Blackout on East Coast
Koreagate: Congress Investigates Tongsun Park
Virginia Wade and Bjorn Borg Win at Wimbledon
Da Doo Ron Ron—Shaun Cassidy—Song • Studio 54

AUGUST

Lights Out on B'way to Honor the Late Alfred Lunt
Space Shuttle *Enterprise* Taken Aloft on Back of 747
*I Claudius, Washington: Behind Closed Doors, Centennial,
Wheels,* & *How the West Was Won*—TV

SEPTEMBER

New Treaty Will Return Panama Canal to Panama
Canada and US Agree to Build Alaska-US Pipeline
Annie & *Beatlemania*—B'way Musicals • *On Our Own*—TV
Blue Bayou—Linda Ronstadt—Song • *Oh God!*—Movie

OCTOBER

Yankees and Reggie Jackson Beat Dodgers in World Series
Lou Brock, Portland Trailblazers, Earl Campbell,
Walter Payton, Marquette University Basketball—Sports
Saturday Night Fever—Movie • Top Albums Sell for $7.98

NOVEMBER

6 Million in Transcendental Meditation, 5 Million Yoga
Lakers Airways Cheap Flights • Farrah Fawcett Look
350,000 Cuisinarts • Coffee Goes To $5 Lb • Moog and Arp
Tonight's the Night—Song • 15,000 Discos • Liquid Protein Diets

DECEMBER

Jimmy Carter, Anwar Sadat, Hubert Humphrey,
Billy Graham, Gerald Ford, Henry Kissinger,
Menachem Begin, Ronald Reagan, Pope Paul VI,
Richard Nixon, Bob Hope—Gallup Most Admired

SONGS

Margaritaville
*You Make Me Feel
Like Dancing*
Blinded by the Light
You Light Up My Life

MOVIES

Annie Hall
Smokey and the Bandit
*Close Encounters of
the Third Kind*
The Goodbye Girl
Looking for Mr Goodbar

BOOKS

*The Grass Is Always
Greener Over
the Septic Tank*
Oliver's Story
Gnomes
Haywire
Book of Lists

1978

HEADLINES

1st Test Tube Baby

Jim Jones Cult
    Deaths in Guyana

2 Popes Die in One Year

Proposition 13 Cuts
    Taxes in California

Troubles Brewing in
    Iran and Nicaragua

Supreme Court
    Bakke Decision

JANUARY

US and Japan Agree to Balance Trade Between Countries
NASA Recruits 35 New Astronauts, 6 Women, 3 Blacks
Soviet Nuclear Spy Satellite Crashes in Canada
Baby Come Back—Song • *Scruples*—Book

FEBRUARY

Carter Wants 24% More for Federal Education
Civil War Begins in Nicaragua • *Short People*—Song
Dolly Parton—Country Music Entertainer of the Year
Judge Says Girls Can't Be Barred from Boys' Sports

MARCH

Tanker *Amoco Cadiz* Sinks, Worst Oil Spill to Date
US Trade Deficit Highest Ever • *Night Fever*—Song
*Barney Miller, Dukes of Hazzard, Waverly Wonders,
Barnaby Jones, Soap, CHIPS,* & *Eight Is Enough*—TV

APRIL

Carter Raises Retirement Age from 60 to 70
President Puts off Work on the Neutron Bomb
52 Million Shares Sold on Stock Market's Heaviest Day
Because the Night—Song • *Bloodline*—Sidney Sheldon—Book

MAY

UN Condemns Actions of South Africa and Apartheid
Senate OKs Selling Fighter Planes to Israel and Arabs
Legalized Casinos Open in Atlantic City, New Jersey
1st Class Stamp Goes from 13¢ to 15¢ • *Feels So Good*—Song

JUNE

Spy Bugs Found in Chimney of US Embassy Moscow
Grease—Movie • Affirmed Wins the Triple Crown
Mopeds • Toga Parties • Jogging and Jogging Suits
Widespread Rumors of a Human Clone • *BJ and the Bear*—TV

1978

JULY

Price of Gold Goes Over $200 per Ounce
Supreme Court Allows Offshore Drilling on East Coast
With a Little Luck & *Shadow Dancing*—Songs
The Far Pavillions—Book • *The Buddy Holly Story*—Movie

AUGUST

Carter Signs Bill, NYC to Get $1.6 Billion in Loans
3 US Balloonists Cross Atlantic from Maine to France
US Congress Votes to End Aid to Somoza in Nicaragua
Miss You—Song • *Heaven Can Wait*—Movie • *Illusions*—Book

SEPTEMBER

Carter Leads Camp David Accords Between
Sadat and Begin to Bring Peace in Middle East
Keith Moon Dies • *Death on the Nile*—Movie
Muhammed Ali Beats Leon Spinks, Wins Crown 3rd Time

OCTOBER

Reminiscing & *Hot Child in the City*—Songs
Yankees Win Series: Bob Welch vs Mr October
Bad Week on Wall Street: Dow Drops 59 Points to 838
Federal Reserve Board Raises Prime Rate to 9.55% to Stem Inflation

NOVEMBER

Cult in Guyana Murders California Representative
Leo Ryan and then Commits Mass Suicide
San Francisco Mayor and Supervisor Harvey Milk Murdered
Some Girls, Don't Look Back, & *52nd Street*—Albums

DECEMBER

Cleveland 1st City to Default Since Depression
Texas Instruments Introduces the Speak and Spell
You Don't Bring Me Flowers—Diamond and Streisand—Song
Foul Play, High Anxiety, & *Midnight Express*—Movies

SONGS

Stayin' Alive
Running on Empty
Love Is Thicker
Than Water

MOVIES

The Deerhunter
Animal House
Coming Home
Superman
Days of Heaven

BOOKS

Mommie Dearest
The Complete Book
of Running
My Mother, My Self
Jackie Oh!

1979

JANUARY

Le Freak, My Life, & *I Love the Night Life*—Songs
Women Body Builders • Jeep Wagoneer 4-Wheel Drive
Mork & Mindy, Laverne & Shirley, & *Happy Days*—TV
Bella Abzug Fired from Advisory Committee on Women

FEBRUARY

Carter Visits Mexico, Interested in Their Oil
Protesting Farmers Drive Assorted Vehicles into DC
US Ambassador to Afghanistan Kidnapped, Murdered
Da Ya Think I'm Sexy, Y.M.C.A., & *Little More Love*—Songs

MARCH

Three Mile Island Nuclear Accident Forces Evacuation
I Will Survive, Tragedy, Fire, & *Heaven Knows*—Songs
Voyager 1 Passes near Jupiter • *China Syndrome*—Movie
The Jordache Look—Designer Jeans • King Tut Exhibition

APRIL

Congress Raises National Debt Ceiling to $830 Billion
Carter Launches Campaign to Ratify SALT Treaty
"Danskins Are Not Just for Dancing"—Ad • *Reunited*—Song
Acid Rain • Gasahol • Black Holes • Interferon • Hot Tubs

MAY

George Bush Announces He's Running for President
65,000 People at Nuclear Protest in Washington DC
$10.5 Million Awarded to Estate of Karen Silkwood
Pritikin Program & *Complete Scarsdale Diet*—Books

JUNE

Carter OKs MX Missile System That Will Cost $33 Billion
Brezhnev and Carter Sign SALT II Nuclear Treaty
OPEC Countries Announce 50% Hike in Oil Prices
Odd-Even Gasoline Sales Start in NY, Other States Follow

HEADLINES

Three Mile Island

US and Red China
Establish Diplomatic
Relations

Russians Invade
Afghanistan

Sandinistas Take
Nicaragua,
Somoza Out

American Hostages
Taken in Iran

Pittsburgh Wins
Superbowl and
World Series

1979

JULY

Carter Limits Public Buildings' Air Conditioning to 78°
Skylab Space Station Crashes in Australia • *Vega$*—TV
Price of Gold Rises to Over $300 Ounce • Roller Disco
Chuck E's in Love, Bad Girls, & *Ring My Bell*—Songs

AUGUST

Yankee Catcher Thurman Munson Killed in Plane Crash
Justice Dept Sues Philadelphia for Police Brutality
USSR Dancer Alexander Godunov Seeks Asylum in US
WKRP in Cincinnati—TV • *Love at First Bite*—Movie

SEPTEMBER

Mexico Will Sell Natural Gas to US Companies
The Jerk, The Main Event, & *The Life of Brian*—Movies
45,000 Public School Teachers on Strike • *Rise*—Song
Sugar Babies—B'way • *Alien*—Movie • *Jailbird*—Book

OCTOBER

Nobel Peace Prize Awarded to Mother Teresa of India
Pope John Paul II Tours US, 20% of Country Catholic
Don't Stop 'til You Get Enough, Sad Eyes, & *Sail On*—Songs
Shah of Iran Has Surgery in NY Hospital • *Pop Muzik*—Song

NOVEMBER

Ronald Reagan Announces Presidential Candidacy
Iranian Militants Take US Embassy and 54 Hostages
Carter Bans Oil Imports from Iran, Seizes Their Assets
Report Says US Vietnam Troops Exposed to Agent Orange

DECEMBER

11 Dead, 28 Injured at Rock Concert in Cincinnati
Senate Approves $1.5 Billion Loan to Chrysler
Clergymen Visit Iran Hostages in 50th Day of Captivity
Pittsburgh's Steelers and Pirates Champs! • Carter Runs Again

SONGS

My Sharona
We Are Family
Too Much Heaven
Knock on Wood
Heart of Glass
Forever in Blue Jeans

MOVIES

10—Bo Derek
  and Dudley Moore
Apocalypse Now
Kramer vs Kramer
Norma Rae
Manhattan
Being There
Rock and Roll
  High School

BOOKS

How to Prosper During
  the Coming Bad Years
Anatomy of an Illness
Lauren Bacall by Myself
Cruel Shoes
  —Steve Martin

1980

HEADLINES

High Inflation

John Lennon Dead

Iran and Iraq at War

ABSCAM Sting
   Catches Politicians

US Ice Hockey Team
   Beats Russians and
   Wins Gold at
   Winter Olympics

Dallas—TV
   Who Shot JR?

JANUARY

Carter OKs Weapons Sale to Red China
Canadians Help 6 Americans Escape from Iran
Price of Gold Peaks at $850 Ounce, Silver $48 Ounce
US Embargo on Grain and High Tech, Soviets Are Mad

FEBRUARY

New Mexico Authorities Recapture the Prison at
Santa Fe after Bloody Riot: 33 Killed, 89 Wounded
40 Million Acres Held for Wildlife Refuge in Alaska
Three's Company, Taxi, Alice, & *Trapper John, MD*—TV

MARCH

Silver Price Drop Threatens Hunt Brothers' Fortune
Limit on Federally Insured Accounts Raised to $100,000
Ford Says Reagan Can't Win Election, Offers Himself
Freedom Sails for US and *America's* Cup • *The Wall*—Pink Floyd

APRIL

US Raid to Rescue Hostages in Iran Fails, 8 Die
Olympics Committee: US to Boycott Olympics in USSR
Many Large Banks Raise Prime Lending Rate to 20%
Call Me, Ride Like the Wind, & *Special Lady*—Songs

MAY

Mount St Helens Erupts in Washington State, 26 Dead
Rioting in Miami after Black Executive Is Slain
Sensory Deprivation Tanks • *Sexy Eyes*—Song
Datsuns Talk to Their Drivers • *White Shadow*—TV

JUNE

OPEC Continues to Raise Prices of Crude Oil
Supreme Court Says Biological Organisms Can Be Patented
Princess Daisy & *Rage of Angels*—Best-selling Novels
The Rose, Fame, & *Urban Cowboy*—Movies • Häagen Daz

1980

JULY
Men Born in 1960 and 1961 Must Register for Draft
Republican Convention in Detroit Nominates Reagan
Billy Carter Suspected as Libyan Agent by Senate
Little Jeannie & *Shining Star*—Songs • *Caddyshack*—Movie

_____

_____

AUGUST
Democrats Nominate Carter and Mondale in NYC
George Brett, Ron Cey, Steve Carlton—Baseball
Lech Walesa Leads Solidarity, New Polish Trade Union
Upside Down—Song • *Little Gloria . . . Happy at Last*—Book

_____

_____

SEPTEMBER
White House Years—Kissinger, *The Real War*—Nixon
Will: Autobiography of G. Gordon Liddy—Books
The Jeffersons, That's Incredible, & *Real People*—TV
Castro Closes Cuban Port from Which 125,000 Have Fled

_____

_____

OCTOBER
House Expels Member for ABSCAM, 1st Since 1861
Dungeons and Dragons—Game • *Woman in Love*—Song
Fiscal Budget Deficit Is $59 Billion • Sony Walkman
Viewers Choose Reagan over Carter in National TV Debate

_____

_____

NOVEMBER
Heavens Gate—Mega Movie—Opens and Flops
Ronald Reagan Wins in Landslide over Jimmy Carter
MGM Grand Hotel Fire, Las Vegas, 84 Dead, 100s Hurt
Maidenform Woman: "You'll Never Know Where She'll Turn Up"

_____

_____

DECEMBER
The Electric Horseman—Movie • *Hee Haw*—TV
3 Nuns and Layperson Killed in El Salvador, US Will Cut Aid
John Lennon, 40, Shot Outside The Dakota, New York City
Prime Lending Rate Climbs to 21.5% • US Population: 226

_____

_____

SONGS

Another Brick in the Wall
Magic
Please Don't Go
Rock with You
Crazy Little Thing Called Love
Sailing

MOVIES

The Elephant Man
Ordinary People
Coal Miner's Daughter
Raging Bull
Airplane
Private Benjamin

BOOKS

Thy Neighbor's Wife
Bourne Identity
The Ninja
Men in Love
Dead Zone and *Firestarter* (both by Stephen King)

1981

JANUARY

Carter Approves $5 Million Arms to El Salvador
Ferdinand Marcos Eases Martial Law in Philippines
We Are Not "Doomed to an Inevitable Decline",
Reagan's Inaugural Speech • *Starting Over*—Song

FEBRUARY

Fire at Hilton Hotel in Las Vegas, 8 Die, 200 Injured
Toyota, VW, Mazda, Americans Buying Small Cars
GM and Ford to Institute Largest Rebate Plans Ever
I Love a Rainy Night—Song • Jelly Beans Popular

HEADLINES

Iranian Hostages
Released on Reagan's
Inauguration Day

Reagan Shot

Pope John Paul II Shot

Anwar Sadat Shot
and Killed

Major League Baseball
Strike

Sandra Day O'Connor
1st Woman on
Supreme Court

MARCH

Reagan Submits $695 Billion Budget, $45 Billion Deficit
Walter Cronkite Replaced by Dan Rather on CBS News
Beverly Hills Diet—Book • *Keep On Loving You*—Song
President Shot by John Hinckley in Waschington DC, 3 Others Hurt

APRIL

Justice Dept Announces 30% US Homes Hit by Crime
Successful Maiden Flight of Space Shuttle *Columbia*
Reagan Moves to End 35 Air Quality Controls on Cars
Nice Girls Do—Book • *Any Which Way You Can*—Movie

MAY

Cleveland's Leonard Barker Pitches Perfect Game
Census Bureau Says 28% More Seniors than in 1970
Jet Crashes into Carrier USS *Nimitz*, 14 Men Killed
Angel of the Morning & *Kiss on My List*—Songs

JUNE

Stripes—Movie • *A Woman Needs Love*—Song
Man Arrested in Murders of Atlanta Black Youths
Supreme Court Rules Men-Only Draft Constitutional
Unemployment Rising • *All Those Years Ago*—Song

1981

JULY Hyatt Regency, Kansas City Walkways Collapse, 113 Die
California Sprays For Medfly Despite Health Protests
Chrysler Has $11.6 Million Profit After 2 Bad Years
Jesse's Girl, The One That You Love, & *Elvira*—Songs

AUGUST Baseball Strike Ends • *Endless Love*—Song
Air Trafffic Controllers Union (PATCO) Goes on Strike
Reagan Fires all PATCO Members Who Refuse to Work
US to Produce Neutron Bombs • *Cinderella Complex*—Book

SEPTEMBER Surgery Performed on Embryos
US to Spend Up to $200 Million on Laser Weaponry
Pocket-Sized TV Introduced • *For Your Eyes Only*—Song
Senate Raises Federal Debt to Over $1Trillion • *Gorky Park*—Book

OCTOBER Reagan Asks for 100 MX Missiles and More B-1 Bombers
Fernando Valenzuela and Dodgers Beat Yankees in Series
Superman II—Movie • *Start Me Up* & *Step by Step*—Songs
Confederacy of Dunces & *In the Belly of the Beast*—Books

NOVEMBER *Arthur*—Movie • Sinclair Computer $140
Noble House & *Hotel New Hampshire*—Best-selling Books
Jean Harris Gets 15 Years in Scarsdale Diet Doctor Slaying
First Class Stamp Raised to 20¢ • *Arthur's Theme* Tops Music Charts

DECEMBER Auto Makers Claim Worst Sales Year Since 1961
Strawberry Shortcake Products • Rubik's Cube
Most US Banks Lower Prime Lending Rate to 15¾%
Woman of the Year—B'way • *Answer as a Man*—Book

SONGS

Physical
Bette Davis Eyes
Private Eyes
The Tide Is High
Just the Two of Us

MOVIES

Raiders of the Lost Ark
Chariots of Fire
9 to 5
Absence of Malice
Body Heat

BOOKS

Cosmos
Clan of the Cave Bear
*Miss Piggy's Guide
   to Life*
The White Hotel
The Glitter Dome
Cujo
Side Effects
   —Woody Allen

1982

JANUARY

Reagan Speech Calls for "New Federalism"
Air Florida 737 Crashes into the Potomac in DC
Claus Von Bulow on Trial for Attempted Murder of Wife
Phone Deregulation, AT&T Must Sell Bell Companies

FEBRUARY

Wayne Gretzky Sets a Hockey Scoring Record
Alexander Haig and Reagan Say US Will Aid El Salvador
Reagan Calls for Strengthening of Nation's Defenses
I Love Rock and Roll—Song • *Torch Song Trilogy*—Play

HEADLINES

Argentina and Britain
  Fight over
  Falkland Islands

General Dozier
  Rescued in Italy

Beirut Massacre

Brezhnev Dies,
  Andropov Takes Over

DeLorean Arrested
  for Cocaine

Tylenol Laced with
  Cyanide Kills 7
  in Chicago

Football Strike

MARCH

John Belushi Dies from Drugs in Hollywood Hotel
Missing, Quest for Fire, & *Neighbors*—Movies
Space Shuttle *Columbia* Goes into Orbit for 3rd Time
Calvin Klein Designer Underwear • *Cheers*—TV

APRIL

Reagan Sides with Britain in Falkland Islands War
Home Computers and Energy-Saving Appliances Selling Well
Master of the Game—Book • *Diner*—Movie • Deely Bobbers
Cats—B'way • MTV—Music Videos • Kodak Disc Cameras

MAY

Reagan Attends Opening of Worlds Fair, Knoxville
Spain Joins NATO as 16th Member • *Porky's*—Movie
Cable Television Grows to $4.6 Billion Business
No Bad Dogs—Book • *Freeze Frame*—Song

JUNE

Steven Spielberg's *ET* Opens, Sets Box Office Records
The Equal Rights Amendment (ERA) Fails Ratification
Anti-Nuke Rallies Around US, 500,000 in Central Park
Reagan Addresses Both Houses of English Parliament

1982

JULY

Life Extension—Book—Causes Megavitamin Explosion
Paul Newman's Salad Dressing • Bicycle Motocross
Hard to Say I'm Sorry & *Eye of the Tiger*—Songs
Rev Moon Marries 2,075 Couples in Madison Square Garden

AUGUST

US Unemployment Rate Highest Since WWII at 9.8%
Asbestos Health Threat Plagues Manville Corporation
US Marines Land in Beirut • Last Checker Cabs Built
Valley Girls • Shoulder Pads • Video Arcades • Rap Music

SEPTEMBER

San Francisco Cable Cars Stop, to Be Rebuilt
Princess Grace of Monaco Dies in Auto Accident
Poltergeist, Blade Runner, & *Victor-Victoria*—Movies
Real Men Don't Eat Quiche & *Jane Fonda's Workout*—Books

OCTOBER

Jack and Diane, Hard to Say I'm Sorry, & *Truly*—Songs
USA Today—National Newspaper • *Rocky III*—Movie
ET Dolls and Products Selling • Disney's EPCOT Opens
Inversion Boots—Exercise Fad • *Mickey*— Song • Smurfs

NOVEMBER

US Marines Patroling Christian Sector in Beirut
Veterans in DC for Unveiling of Vietnam Memorial
Making Love, Abracadabra, & *Ebony & Ivory*—Songs
Football Strike Over • *Reds, Frances, Taps,* & *48 Hours*—Movies

DECEMBER

Barney Clark Receives Artificial (Jarvik) Heart
Last Raggedy Ann Dolls • *Gloria* & *Heart Attack*—Songs
Biggest Cash Robbery Yet: $5.3 Million in Bronx, NY
Senator Edward Kennedy Says He Will Not Run for President

SONGS

Centerfold
Don't You Want Me
Who Can It Be Now?
Up Where We Belong

MOVIES

Gandhi
On Golden Pond
The World According to Garp
An Officer and a Gentleman

BOOKS

Light in the Attic
A Few Minutes with Andy Rooney
Living, Loving, and Learning
Valley of the Horses
At Dawn We Slept

1983

JANUARY

US and USSR Resume Arms Talks in Geneva
4 Storms Hit California Coast, 11 Dead, Costs $70 Million
Truckers Strike to Protest High Taxes on Diesel Fuel
Queen Elizabeth Tours US West Coast • *Cagney & Lacey*—TV

FEBRUARY

Mid-Atlantic Paralyzed by Winter Storm, 15 Killed
United American Bank Fails • *Down Under*—Song
GM and Toyota Agree to Build Compact Cars in US
Punks Are Slam Dancing • Computer Hackers

HEADLINES

Russians Shoot Down
Korean Airliner

Bomb Kills 237 Marines
in Beirut

Lech Walesa Gets Nobel
Peace Prize

Australia II Wins
America's Cup

Klaus Barbie Caught and
Returned to France

James Watt, "I Have
a Black, I Have
a Woman, Two
Jews, and a Cripple."

MARCH

OPEC Agrees to Cut Oil Prices from $34 to $29 a Barrel
Thorn Birds—TV Miniseries, Mr T on *The A-Team*—TV
Stray Cat Strut & *Hungry Like the Wolf*—Songs
Anne Burford Resigns as EPA Head • *The Verdict*—Movie

APRIL

US Space Shuttle *Challenger* Flies on Maiden Launch
Harold Washington Becomes 1st Black Mayor of Chicago
Germans Claim to Have Hitler Diaries, They Prove Fake
Beat It & *Do You Really Want to Hurt Me?*—Songs

MAY

AIDS Is the #1 Priority of US Public Health Service
Nicaragua Expels 3 US Diplomats • *Let's Dance*—Song
Huge Celebration for Brooklyn Bridge 100th Birthday
US Hosts Economic Summit in Williamsburg, VA

JUNE

Dr Sally Ride Becomes 1st US Woman in Space
Joan Rivers—Permanent Guest Host on *The Tonight Show*
New Stock Market High: Dow Jones 1,248.30
Japanese Asexual Clothes • *Creating Wealth*—Book

1983

JULY
James Watt Bans Beach Boys from 4th of July Concert
Reagan Proposes Amendment Allowing School Prayer
Reagan Denies Plans of War in South America
In Search of Excellence—Book • *Maniac*—Song

AUGUST
Hottest August on Record Causes 22 Deaths
Flashdance—Movie—Torn Sweatshirts Are Fashionable
Sweet Dreams Are Made of This & *Electric Avenue*—Songs
Maureen Reagan Tries to Help Father's Image with Women

SEPTEMBER
Congress Allows Reagan to Keep Marines in Beirut
The Karate Kid, Star 80, Yentl, & *Sophie's Choice*—Movies
Unemployment Down to 9.3% • *My One and Only*—B'way
Heartburn, Lonesome Gods, & *Mistral's Daughter*—Novels

OCTOBER
NY Metropolitan Opera Celebrates 100th Anniversary
US Troops Invade and Capture the Island of Grenada
Scarecrow and Mrs King—TV • *Zelig*—Movie
Baby Come to Me, Shame on the Moon, & *Africa*—Songs

NOVEMBER
President Reagan Visits Japan and South Korea
NOW Feminist Ginny Foat Acquitted of Murder
The Day After—TV—Shows Consequences of Nuclear War
Terms of Endearment—Movie • *Uptown Girl*—Song

DECEMBER
Syria Attacks Beirut Airport, 8 Marines Die
Say Say Say—Michael Jackson and Paul McCartney—Song
Compact Discs • Wacky Wallwalkers • Break Dancing
Cabbage Patch Dolls • *Garfield* & *Heathcliffe*—Cartoon Cats

SONGS

What a Feeling
*She Works Hard
  for the Money*
Billie Jean
Every Breath You Take
All Night Long

MOVIES

Tender Mercies
The Big Chill
The Right Stuff
Tootsie
Risky Business

BOOKS

Megatrends
Name of the Rose
Hollywood Wives
One-Minute Manager
Poland and *Space*
  (both by Michener)
Ironweed

1984

JANUARY

Raiders Massacre Redskins in Superbowl XVIII
Hill Street Blues—TV • *Gremlins*—Movie
Say It Isn't So & *Owner of a Lonely Heart*—Songs
Ronald Reagan Will Run Again • Nonalcoholic Beers

FEBRUARY

US Marines Complete Withdrawal from Lebanon
Gary Hart Wins Democratic Primary in New Hampshire
Michael Jackson Burnt While Making Pepsi TV Ad
Karma Chameleon, Jump, & *99 Luftballoons*—Songs

MARCH

Bozo the Clown, Larry Harmon, Runs for President
Guggenheim Museum Shows Picasso's Last Decade
Falcon Crest, Knots Landing, & *Magnum PI*—TV
Michael Jackson's *Thriller* Album Wins 8 Grammys

APRIL

Reports Say CIA Mined Nicaraguan Harbors
Baltimore Colts Move Overnight to Indianapolis
Marvin Gaye Shot by Father • *Against All Odds*—Song
David Kennedy Dead from Drugs • *Footloose*—Song—Movie

MAY

Worlds Fair Opens in New Orleans • *Hello*—Song
President Reagan Leads Tribute to Soldiers Killed in Vietnam
Olympic Torch Relay • Trivial Pursuit • Aerobics
McMartin School, Child Abuse Allegations in Los Angeles

JUNE

Jesse Jackson Gets 22 American Prisoners out of Cuba
Racehorse Swale Wins at Belmont, Dies 8 Days Later
Congress Wants All States to Raise Drinking Age to 21
Celtics NBA Champs Again • VCRs and Video Rentals

HEADLINES

Woman Runs for
Vice President

Famine in Africa

Star Wars, SDI,
Arms in Space

Nation Prays
for Baby Fae

Indira Gandhi
Assassinated

Russians Boycott
Summer Olympics

Industrial Accidents:
Natural Gas
Mexico City
Poison Gas
Bhopal, India

Desmond Tutu Wins
Nobel Peace Prize

1984

JULY
Miss America Gives Up Crown Because of Nude Photos
McDonald's Massacre in San Ysidro, California, 20 Dead
Democrats Nominate Walter Mondale and Geraldine Ferraro
When Doves Cry—Song • Michael Jackson Victory Tour

AUGUST
15.3% of Americans in Poverty • "Where's the Beef?"
Reagan and Bush GOP Nominees • DeLorean Acquitted
XXIII Summer Olympiad in Los Angeles, US Wins Big
with Carl Lewis, Mary Lou Retton, and Men's Gymnastics Team

SEPTEMBER
Police Academy & *Moscow on Hudson*—Movies
US Embassy Bombed in Beirut • *Nothing Down*—Book
Mondale Claims Reagan's Made World More Dangerous
What's Love Got to Do with It—Song • Kids Buying GoBots

OCTOBER
Peter Uberroth Is New Commissioner of Baseball
Reagan and Mondale Begin Series of Debates
Bush and Ferraro Hold First Ever VP Debate on TV
Tofu and Light Foods • *Eat to Win*—Book • Health Clubs

NOVEMBER
Stalin's Daughter, Svetlana, Returns to USSR
Reagan Wins Landslide Victory • *Let's Go Crazy*—Song
Velma Barfield, 1st US Woman Executed in 22 Years
Fashion Has Women Wearing Big Shirts and Men's Underwear

DECEMBER
Bernard Goetz Shoots 4 Teenagers on NY Subway
2,000 Dead in Union Carbide Plant Disaster, India
Jewel in the Crown—PBS TV • *Out of Touch*—Song
Terminator—Movie • *Loving Each Other*—Book

SONGS

Like a Virgin
*Girls Just Want to
Have Fun*
Let's Hear It for the Boy
*I Just Called to Say I
Love You*
Time After Time

MOVIES

Amadeus
Beverly Hills Cop
Purple Rain
The Killing Fields
Ghostbusters
Romancing the Stone

BOOKS

*. . . And Ladies of
the Club*
Lincoln
*Butter Battle Book
—Dr Seuss*
Pet Sematary
*Wired: Biography of
John Belushi*
Walking Drum

1985

JANUARY

The Wild Boys—Song • Bill Cosby TV Show #1
Procter and Gamble Puts Diamonds in Spic & Span Boxes
SF 49ers Beat MiamiDolphins—Superbowl • Dove Bars
US Ignores World Court Proceedings on Nicaragua

FEBRUARY

Missing Kids' Photos on Milk Cartons
USFL Starts 3rd Training Season with Teams Folding
New Zealand Bars US Ships with Nuclear Weapons
Big 3 Auto Makers, $9.8 Bill Profit in 1984 • *Lover Boy*—Song

MARCH

Thousands Lose in Ohio Savings & Loan Default
Russians Shoot US Major Taking Pictures in East Germany
Larry Holmes Wins Final Bout, Announces Retirement
Reeboks—Fashion • *Careless Whisper* & *Lover Girl*—Songs

APRIL

Congress Nixes Contra Military Aid • Swatch Watches
Amy Carter Arrested Protesting Apartheid • Cajun Food
If Tomorrow Comes—Book • *Moonlighting*—TV • Yuppies
We Are the World—Song—Heard Worldwide • Organizer Books

MAY

Bruce Springsteen Marries in Secret Ceremony
LA Lakers Win Basketball Championship from Celtics
EF Hutton Guilty of Illegal Use of Checking Accounts
Glory Days—Song • Navy Family Accused of Selling Secrets to USSR

JUNE

Reagan Says US Will Stay Within SALT II Restrictions
Rambo: First Blood Part II & *The Breakfast Club*—Movies
Millions Watch *Late Night* with David Letterman after Carson
Stirrup Pants • *Iacocca*—Autobiography • *Amazing Stories*—TV

HEADLINES

$400M Treasure
Found in Sunken
Spanish Galleon

Mengeles' Body
Found in Brazil

Rock Hudson Dies
of AIDS

Halley's Comet Returns

Gorbachev Heads USSR

Mexico City Hit
by Earthquake

Reagan Visits
Germany's
Bitburg Cemetery

1985

JULY

Reagan and Gorbachev Hold Summit in Geneva
Boris Becker Youngest to Win at Wimbledon
New Coke Flops, Coca-Cola Brings Back Classic Coke
Live Aid Concert—London and Philadelphia

AUGUST

Miami Vice—TV—Receives 15 Emmy Nominations
President Reagan Has a Patch of Skin Removed from Nose
Falcon and the Snowman—Movie • *Material Girl*—Song
Delta Air Crash in Dallas, 137 Dead • Madonna Look

SEPTEMBER

Farm Aid Concert with Willie Nelson and Others
Reagan Announces More Sanctions Against S Africa
NY Parents Try to Keep Child with AIDS Out of School
Pete Rose Breaks Ty Cobb's Record with 4,192 Base Hits

OCTOBER

Cruise Ship *Achille Lauro* Hijacked, American Killed
US Forces Down Egyptian Airliner with the Terrorists
All Missouri World Series—Royals Beat Cardinals
Woman Joins Harlem Globetrotters • *Mask*—Movie

NOVEMBER

Talk of Ratings and Warning Labels on Rock Albums
Lost Whale, Humphrey, Finally Heads back to Pacific
KGB Spy Yurchenko Embarrasses US by Going Home
US Thrills to Visit of Prince Charles and Princess Di

DECEMBER

The Frugal Gourmet —PBS TV & Bestselling Book
256 US Service Men Die When Chartered Jet Crashes
Dow Jones Climbs Over 1,500—A First • Teddy Ruxpin
Color Purple & *Cocoon*—Movies • *Tango Argentino*—B'way

SONGS

Born in the USA
Power of Love
Private Dancer
Smooth Operator
Wake Me Up Before You Go-Go

MOVIES

Out of Africa
Witness
Prizzi's Honor
Back to the Future
Jewel of the Nile

BOOKS

Lake Wobegon Days
The Mammoth Hunters
Hunt for Red October
Lonesome Dove
Yeager
—An Autobiography

1986

JANUARY

Martin Luther King Jr's Birthday a National Holiday
NBC Charges $550,000 for 30-Second Commercials as
Bears with McMahon and "The Fridge" Win Super Bowl
Shuttle Explodes, 7 Astronauts Die, US Watches in Horror

FEBRUARY

Lee Iaccoca Fired as Statue of Liberty Chairman
Ron Reagan Jr in Undies on *Saturday Night Live*
Debi Thomas Wins US Figure Skating Championship
Fit for Life—Diet Book • Garbage Pail Kids • Speed Walking

MARCH

Robert Penn Warren Becomes 1st US Poet Laureate
US Forces Destroy Libyan Gun Boats Off Their Coast
Room with a View—Movie • Fish Ties—Fashion
Golden Girls & *Wheel of Fortune*—TV • *Max Headroom*—Video

APRIL

Reagan Calls Kadafi a "Mad Dog" as US War Planes
Bomb Libya with British Support to Stop Terrorism
Titan Rocket with Spy Satellite Blows Up on Launch
Clint Eastwood Elected Mayor of Carmel, California

MAY

Wrestling Mania Craze with Pro Wrestling on TV
Jane Fonda's Workout & *Beverly Hills Cop*—Top Videos
Joan Rivers to Leave *The Tonight Show* for Her Own Show
Hands Across America • *Missionary Man*—Song

JUNE

Reagan Chooses William Rehnquist as Chief Justice
Athletes Len Bias and John Rogers Die from Cocaine
Amnesty International Concert Tour in New Jersey
In Los Angeles FBI Agent Is Convicted of Spying for Russians

HEADLINES

Challenger Tragedy

Tax Reform Law Passes

Chernobyl Accident

Baby Doc Duvalier
Flees Haiti

Marcos Ousted
from Philippines

Nancy Reagan Leads
War on Drugs

Crack, Heroin, and
Designer Drugs Scare
the Nation

Nicaragua Releases
Eugene Hasenfus

1986

JULY
Restored Statue of Liberty Unveiled for 100th Birthday
Prince Andrew Weds Fergie • Caroline Kennedy Marries
Greatest Love of All & *Addicted to Love*—Songs
The Monkees Make a Comeback Tour • *Top Gun*—Movie

AUGUST
USFL in Suit Against NFL Awarded $1 in Damages
Greg Lemmond 1st American to Win Tour de France
246 Andrew Wyeth Paintings 1st Seen, All of Helga
California Teenager Turns in Parents for Drug Use

SEPTEMBER
Soviets Arrest Reporter Nick Daniloff for Spying
Oprah Winfrey Show—TV Talk • State Lotteries
Captain EO, 3-D Movie, Michael Jackson, at Disneyland
Nasty & *When I Think of You*—Janet Jackson—Hit Songs

OCTOBER
Mets Beat Boston in 7-Game World Series
Arms Plane Downed in Nicaragua, American Captured
Unauthorized Biography of Frank Sinatra a Bestseller
Harvard Turns 350 • House Votes the Rose Our National Flower

NOVEMBER
Hostage David Jacobsen Released by Lebanese
Bruce Springsteen 1975-1985 Live—Hits Charts at #1
Pet Shop Boys, Bangles, Mr. Mister, Peter Gabriel—Musicians
Boesky Stock Scandal Taints Wall Street • Pound Puppies

DECEMBER
Reagan Under Fire For Iran/Contra Connection
Largest US Cockroach Contest, Winner Gets $1,000
Search for Tomorrow—Oldest Soap Opera—Goes Off TV
Voyager Airplane Flies Nonstop Around the World

SONGS
Higher Love
Graceland
Walk Like an Egyptian
Dancing on the Ceiling
Rock Me Amadeus

MOVIES
Hannah & Her Sisters
Aliens
Star Trek IV
Peggy Sue Got Married
Legal Eagles
Ruthless People

BOOKS
Fatherhood
You're Only Old Once—Dr. Seuss
Women Who Love Too Much
Red Storm Rising
A Day in the Life of America

1987

JANUARY

1st Ads for Condoms on TV, KRON San Francisco
NY Giants Take Super Bowl, Gator Aide Showers for Coach
At This Moment & *Shake You Down*—Songs   •   *Platoon*—Movie
Oral Roberts Says God Will Call Him Home Without $4.5 Million

FEBRUARY

Amerika—TV   •   *Livin' on a Prayer*—Bon Jovi—Song
Dennis Conners and *Stars & Stripes* Regain *America's* Cup
Paperback of Tower Commission Report Is a Bestseller
Liberace Dies in Palm Springs   •   Fawn Hall Testifies Before Congress

HEADLINES

Iraq Attack On
    Destroyer USS *Stark*

Ollie North
    on Witness Stand

Jim Bakker and
    Gary Hart Scandals

Stockmarket:
    1st Time Above 2,000,
    Then 508-Point Crash

3-Year-Old
    Jessica McClure Saved
    from Well in Texas

Mike Tyson
    Heavyweight Champ

MARCH

Mary Beth Whitehead and the Sterns Battle over Baby M
AIDS Drug AZT Approved by Food and Drug Administration
Nothing's Gonna Stop Us Now—Song   •   Indiana Basketball
Hoosiers, Little Shop of Horrors, & *The Mission*—Movies

APRIL

G Gordon Liddy Spends Week on *Super Password*
Dodgers Fire Al Campanis Over *Nightline* Remarks
Genetic Engineering   •   Billionaire Boys Club   •   Clean Water Act
I Knew You Were Waiting—Song   •   British Petroleum Buys Standard Oil

MAY

On *Cheers* Shelly Long Is Replaced by Kirstie Allie
Ted Koppel Interviews Jim and Tammy Bakker on *Nightline*
Michael Jackson Tries to Buy Elephant Man Remains
Ishtar—Movie Bomb   •   Joan Rivers Leaves Own Late Nite TV Show

JUNE

Madonna Tours World and Sean Penn Goes to Jail
I Want to Dance with Somebody, Always, & *Head to Toe*—Songs
Kurt Waldheim Denied Entry to US over Wartime Nazi Ties
Hurdler Edwin Moses Loses a Race After 122 Wins

1987

JULY

Homeless Garbage Barge Cruises East Coast from NY to Florida
Freeway Shootings and Joan Collins Divorce Trial in LA
French Explorers Bring Up Dishes from the Titanic
Nuts, Black Widow, The Princess Bride, & *Full Metal Jacket*—Movies

_____

_____

_____

AUGUST

Little Cecila Only Survivor in Detroit Air Crash
Harmonic Convergence • Pan American Games in Indianapolis
NY Stock Market Reaches Record 2722.42 • *La Bamba*—Song
Elvis Sightings, 10,000 at Graceland on 10th Anniversary of Death

_____

_____

_____

SEPTEMBER

Pope Tours US • *Thirtysomething*—TV
Bob Woodward Interview with Dying William Casey
Fully Clothed Jerry Falwell Rides Water Slide at PTL Park
Michael Jackson Tours Japan • Dan Rather Walks Off Set

_____

_____

_____

OCTOBER

Stock Market Drops 508 Points in 1 Day
Here I Go Again & *Bad*—Songs • Senate Rejects Bork
Jesse Jackson, Pat Robertson, and George Bush Are Running
Who's That Girl?—Song • Earthquake in LA • US Bombs Offshore Iran

_____

_____

_____

NOVEMBER

I Think We're Alone Now—Tiffany—Song
2nd Court Nominee Admits Pot Smoke, 3rd Anthony Kennedy
Cuban Prisoners in US Riot • Van Gogh's *Irises* Gets $50 Million
Sony Buys CBS Records • Tania Aebi Ends Solo Sail Round World

_____

_____

_____

DECEMBER

Passengers Fighting Over Airline Smoking Bans
Faith—George Michael—Song • Dalkon Shield Ban
Gorbachev Jumps from Limo to Mingle with Everyday Americans
Ollie Doll Out, Gorby Doll In • *Les Miserables*—B'way

_____

_____

_____

SONGS

The Time of My Life
*I Still Haven't Found
  What I'm Looking For*
*Didn't We Almost
  Have It All?*
*You Have to Fight for
  Your Right to Party*

MOVIES

The Last Emperor
Good Morning Vietnam
Broadcast News
Moonstruck
Three Men and a Baby

BOOKS

*The Bonfire of the
  Vanities*
Presumed Innocent
The Art of the Deal
  —Donald Trump
Cultural Literacy

1988

JANUARY

George Bush Chides Dan Rather about Walking Off Set
The Phantom of the Opera—B'way • *Raising Arizona*—Movie
CBS Fires Jimmy "the Greek" • *So Emotional* & *Could've Been*—Songs
Seabrook Nuclear Power Plant Bankrupt • Pittsburgh Oil Spill

HEADLINES

Hollywood
   Writers Strike

Fax Machines

Meese Resigns

Iranian Airliner
   Shot Down

Pentagon Procurement
   Scandals

Pan Am Flight 103
   Blows Up
   Over Lockerbie

FEBRUARY

"I have sinned" Sobs Jimmy Swaggart on TV
Japanese Buy Firestone Tires • *Au Revoir les Enfants*—Movie
Calgary Winter Olympic Games Star Brian Boitano,
Bonnie Blair, Eddie the Eagle, and the Jamaican Bobsled Team

MARCH

Tougher Than Leather—Run DMC— Album
US Troops to Honduras on Rumored Nicaraguan Invasion
Goddess of Love—Vanna White—TV • Susan Butcher—Iditarod Race
Deaf Students at Gallaudet College Demand and Get Deaf President

APRIL

Arizona Governor Mecham Removed from Office
Where Do Broken Hearts Go?—Whitney Houston—Song
Sonny Bono Palm Springs Mayor and Cher Wins Oscar
Arena Football • Baltimore Orioles Finally Win a Game

MAY

Tom Selleck in Final *Magnum PI* • *Wishing Well*—Song
Michael Jordan Scores 55 in Basketball Playoffs
Don Regan's *For the Record* Claims Astrologer Advised White House
Irving Berlin is 100 • Navy Must Review Safety Procedures

JUNE

Disposable Cameras • US Drought • *Dirty Diana*—Song
Yankees Fire Billy Martin for 5th Time • LA Lakers 2 in a Row
Wizard of Oz Slippers $165,000 at Auction • *Starlight Express*—B'way
Tracy Chapman—Album • *Night Court*—TV • *Big*—Movie

1988

JULY   *The Wonder Years*—TV • David Hockney Exhibit Tours US
Reagan Signs Catastrophic Health Care Bill • Last Playboy Club
Medical Wastes on Eastern Beaches • North Sea Oil Rig Explosion
Last Temptation of Christ Draws Protests • Yellowstone Park Fires

---

AUGUST   Pledge of Allegiance Campaign Issue • *Roll with It*—Song
1st Night Game Wrigley Field • Wayne Gretzky to LA Kings
Rupert Murdoch Buys *TV Guide* • Rogaine for Hair Growth
Crocodile Dundee II, Die Hard, Coming to America, & *Beetlejuice*—Movies

---

SEPTEMBER   Bart Giamatti, Dennis Conners, Steffi Graf
José Canseco, Tim Browning, Greg Lougainis—Sports
Accidents Revealed at Savanah Nuclear Plant • Radon Gas
Don't Worry, Be Happy, Hysteria, & *Appetite for Destruction*—Music

---

OCTOBER   Bentsen Tells Quayle "You're No Jack Kennedy!"
Combined Effort to Save Whales Trapped in Arctic Ice
Trump Buys Eastern Shuttle • *Battlecry of Freedom*—Book
Orel Hershiser Record 67 Scoreless Innings • Dodgers Win Series

---

NOVEMBER   George Bush President • Thousand Points of Light
Robin Givens-Mike Tyson Split • B-1 Bombers Grounded
Georgia O'Keeffe Show Tours Country • *Kokomo*—Song
Morton Downey, Sally Jesse Raphaël, Geraldo Rivera, Phil Donahue—Talk TV

DECEMBER   CBS Buys Baseball TV Rights for Next 4 Years
Who Framed Roger Rabbit?, Working Girl, & *Twins*—Movies
Armenian Earthquake • Poison Gas Plant in Libya
Bush Hunts Quail in Beeville, Texas • RJR Nabisco Sold, $24 Billion

---

SONGS

Fast Car
One Step Up
Man in the Mirror
Always on My Mind
Behind the Wheel

MOVIES

*The Unbearable
  Lightness of Being*
Bull Durham
The Naked Gun
Dirty Rotten Scoundrels

BOOKS

*All I Really Need to Know
  I Learned in
  Kindergarten*
A Brief History of Time
Chaos
*The Cardinal
  of the Kremlin*

1989

JANUARY

Warners Pays $25 Million for *Happy Birthday*
Pat Sajak and Arsenio Hall—Late Night TV
Japanese Emperor Hirohito Dies • Ted Bundy Executed
Two Hearts—Song • *42nd Street*—B'way • *Beaches*—Movie

FEBRUARY

Lonesome Dove—TV • *Mississippi Burning*—Movie
Straight Up—Paula Abdul—Song • Fox TV Network
Ayatollah Sentences Salman Rushdie to Death over Book *Satanic Verses*
135-Year-Old Sailing Record NY to San Francisco Broken by *Thursday's Child*

HEADLINES

Hurricane Hugo

Zsa Zsa Gabor Slaps Cop

Exxon Valdez Oil Spill

Tiananmen Square
   Democracy Movement

San Francisco
   Earthquake

US Invades Panama

The Berlin Wall
   Comes Down

The Failure of
   Communism

MARCH

Madonna Sells Pepsi—George Michael Sells Diet Coke
Miss USA Is from Texas for 5th Year in a Row
Beta-Carotene • Assault Rifles • Michael Millken
Oscar Telecast Featuring Rob Lowe and Snow White Angers Disney

APRIL

Gun Turret Blast Kills 47 on Navy's Battleship *Iowa*
Joy Luck Club—Book • *She Drives Me Crazy*—Song
NY Times Says Cold War Over • Richard Daley Jr, Mayor of Chicago
Anchorwoman Shuffle: Diane Sawyer, Connie Chung, & Mary Alice Williams

MAY

900 Phone Numbers • Lap Top Computers • Alar
Stairmasters • Invitro Fertilization • Voice Mail
1st Tour de Trump American Bicycle Race • *Rock On*—Song
House Speaker Jim Wright Resigns • Sunday Silence—Kentucky Derby

JUNE

Democracy Movement in Tiananmen Square Crushed
"This is not your father's Oldsmobile" "The Heartbeat of America"
Fugitive Wanted Since 1971 Caught Due to *America's Most Wanted*—TV
Florida Girl Sues Boy Who Didn't Show for Prom • Ayatollah Khomeini Dies

116

1989

JULY

Supreme Court Allows Flag Burning, Bush Wants Amendment
Congress Stews Over Censorship and Funding in the Arts
Crippled DC-10 Crash Lands in Sioux City, Iowa, 150 Survive
Batdance—Song • Cholesterol • Cold Fusion • Oat Bran

AUGUST

FBI Sting Catches 46 Chicago Commodity Traders
Wrongfully Accused of Rape, Gary Dotson Gets New Hearing
Disney Buys the Muppets • Poland Ousts Communism
The Rolling Stones, Paul McCartney, and The Who Hit the Road Again

SEPTEMBER

Bush Shows Crack Bought near White House, on TV
Nashville Judge Gives Wife Frozen Embryos in Divorce Case
Marcos Dies in Hawaii • Lexus, Miata, Sterling, Infinity—New Cars
20-Ton Cocaine Bust in LA, Dealers Are the New Hollywood Villains

OCTOBER

Chris Evert, Tom Landry, and Kareem Retire, SF 49ers,
Wrestlemania, Detroit Pistons, Greg Lemond—Sports
Oklahoma Football Team, Pete Rose, Ben Johnson,
Steroids, British Soccer Fans, Dexter Manley—Sports Scandals

NOVEMBER

Batman, Movie Mega Hit Comes Out on Home Video
Minimum Wage to $4.25 • Lincoln Savings & Loan
Lech Walesa before Congress • Germans Dance Atop Berlin Wall
Kirby Puckett Signs for $3 Million • *Nick of Time*—Bonnie Raitt—Album

DECEMBER

50 Simple Thing You Can Do to Save the Earth—Book
Deborah Norville Takes Jane Pauley's Place on *Today Show*
Turmoil in Eastern Europe: Czechoslovakia, Rumania, Hungary
Billy Martin, Samuel Beckett, and Nicolae Ceausecu Dead This Month

SONGS

We Didn't Start the Fire
Rythmn Nation
The Living Years
Another Day in Paradise
I'll Be Loving You

MOVIES

Born on the 4th of July
When Harry Met Sally
Do the Right Thing
Dead Poets Society
Field of Dreams
Driving Miss Daisy
My Left Foot

BOOKS

Clear & Present Danger
Dark Half
Caribbean
*It Was on Fire When I
   Lay Down on It*
It's Always Something

117

1990

JANUARY
Washington DC Mayor Marion Barry Busted for Drugs
The Simpsons—Animation—TV • *Roger and Me*—Movie
Acquittals in McMartin Preschool Molestation Case in Los Angeles
AT&T Software Glitch Cuts Long Distance Phone Calls for 9 Hours

_____

_____

FEBRUARY
Daniel Ortega and Sandinistas Voted Out in Nicaragua
The National—Sports Newspaper • Spring Training Baseball Lockout
McDonald's Opens in Moscow, Hungry Russians Line Up for Blocks
Junk Bond Kings Drexel, Burnham, Lambert File for Bankruptcy

_____

_____

HEADLINES

Noriega Captured and
Brought to US

Buster Douglas Beats
Mike Tyson

Nelson Mandela
Released and
Tours America

Dow Jones Goes Briefly
Above 3,000

Germany to Reunify
and Join NATO

Savings & Loan Crisis

Iraq Invades Kuwait

MARCH
The Caution Horses—The Cowboy Junkies &
Highwayman 2—Cash, Jennings, Kristofferson, and Nelson—Albums
Loyola Marymount Basketball Star Hank Gathers Dies During Game
Hunt for Red October—Movie • *America's Funniest Home Videos*—TV

_____

_____

APRIL
Billion $ Hubble Space Telescope Launched into Orbit
President Shuns Broccoli • Trump's Taj Mahal Opens in Atlantic City
Guns N' Rose's, 2 Live Crew, & NWA Prompt Censorship Questions
Senate Passes Clean Air Bill • Gloria Estefan Injured in Bus Crash

_____

_____

MAY
Cadillac Man, Longtime Companion, & *Bird on a Wire*—Movies
Broken Campaign Promise: Bush Admits He May Raise Taxes
Bourne Ultimatum, Family Pictures, & *September*—Books
Twin Peaks—Who Killed Laura Palmer?—TV • Madonna Tours World

_____

_____

JUNE
Burden of Proof—Scott Turow—Book
Republicans and Democrats Both Tainted by Savings & Loan Scandal
Censorship Controversy Continues with Jesse Helms, the NEA,
Banned Photos, Banned Artists, and Robert Maplethorpe

_____

_____

118

JULY

2 No-Hitters in One Day: Dave Stewart and Fernando Valenzuela
Trump Has Money Troubles: He's on $450,000 Monthly Allowance
Nolan Ryan Wins #300 • George Steinbrenner Out at Yankees
Presumed Innocent & *The Freshman*—Movies • Nixon Museum Opens

_____

_____

_____

AUGUST

The Two Jakes, Air America, & *Mo' Better Blues*—Movies
Iraq Invades Kuwait, Threatening Saudi Arabia and US Oil
Planes, Ships, and Thousands of American Troops Sent to Saudi Arabia
Memories of Midnight—Book • *Wild at Heart*—David Lynch—Movie

_____

_____

_____

SEPTEMBER

_____

_____

_____

OCTOBER

_____

_____

_____

NOVEMBER

_____

_____

_____

DECEMBER

_____

_____

_____

1990

SONGS

Step by Step
Cradle of Love
Enjoy the Silence
When I'm Back on My Feet Again
I Do Not Want What I Haven't Got

MOVIES

Teenage Mutant Ninja Turtles
Pretty Woman
Dick Tracy
Die Hard II
Ghost
Wild at Heart
Godfather III

BOOKS

Oh the Places You'll Go—Dr Seuss
Plains of Passage
Lady Boss
Dazzle
LifeLog: A Celebration of the Twentieth Century

1991 JANUARY

_____
_____
_____

FEBRUARY

HEADLINES

_____
_____
_____

MARCH

_____
_____
_____

APRIL

_____
_____
_____

MAY

_____
_____
_____

JUNE

_____
_____
_____

JULY

_____
_____
_____

AUGUST

_____
_____
_____

SEPTEMBER

_____
_____

OCTOBER

_____
_____
_____

NOVEMBER

_____
_____
_____

DECEMBER

_____
_____
_____

1991

_____

SONGS
_____

MOVIES
_____

BOOKS
_____

1992 JANUARY

_____

_____

_____

FEBRUARY

_____

_____

MARCH

_____

_____

APRIL

_____

_____

MAY

_____

_____

JUNE

_____

_____

_____

JULY

_____

1992

_____

_____
SONGS

AUGUST

_____

_____

_____

SEPTEMBER

_____

_____
MOVIES

_____

OCTOBER

_____

_____

_____

NOVEMBER

_____
BOOKS

_____

_____

DECEMBER

_____

_____

_____

1993 JANUARY

_____
_____

FEBRUARY

HEADLINES

_____
_____

MARCH

_____
_____

APRIL

_____
_____

MAY

_____
_____

JUNE

_____
_____
_____

JULY

1993

_____

_____

SONGS
_____

AUGUST

_____

_____

SEPTEMBER

MOVIES
_____

_____

OCTOBER

_____

_____

NOVEMBER

BOOKS
_____

_____

DECEMBER

_____

_____

_____

1994 JANUARY

_____
_____
_____

FEBRUARY

HEADLINES

_____
_____
_____

MARCH

_____
_____
_____

APRIL

_____
_____
_____

MAY

_____
_____
_____

JUNE

_____
_____
_____

JULY

_____

_____

AUGUST

_____

_____

SEPTEMBER

_____

_____

OCTOBER

_____

_____

NOVEMBER

_____

_____

DECEMBER

_____

_____

_____

1994

SONGS

MOVIES

BOOKS

1995 JANUARY

_____

_____

_____

FEBRUARY

HEADLINES

_____

_____

_____

MARCH

_____

_____

_____

APRIL

_____

_____

_____

MAY

_____

_____

_____

JUNE

_____

_____

_____

JULY

_____
_____
_____

AUGUST

_____
_____
_____

SEPTEMBER

_____
_____

OCTOBER

_____
_____
_____

NOVEMBER

_____
_____

DECEMBER

_____
_____
_____

1995

SONGS

MOVIES

BOOKS

1996 JANUARY

_____
_____
_____

FEBRUARY

HEADLINES

_____
_____
_____

MARCH

_____
_____
_____

APRIL

_____
_____
_____

MAY

_____
_____
_____

JUNE

_____
_____
_____

JULY

1996

SONGS

AUGUST

SEPTEMBER

MOVIES

OCTOBER

NOVEMBER

BOOKS

DECEMBER

1997

JANUARY

_____
_____

HEADLINES

FEBRUARY

_____
_____

MARCH

_____
_____

APRIL

_____
_____

MAY

_____
_____

JUNE

_____
_____
_____

JULY

_____

_____

AUGUST

_____

_____

SEPTEMBER

_____

_____

OCTOBER

_____

_____

NOVEMBER

_____

_____

DECEMBER

_____

_____

_____

1997

SONGS

MOVIES

BOOKS

1998 JANUARY

_____

_____

HEADLINES

FEBRUARY

_____

_____

MARCH

_____

_____

APRIL

_____

_____

MAY

_____

_____

JUNE

_____

_____

JULY

1998

SONGS

AUGUST

SEPTEMBER

MOVIES

OCTOBER

NOVEMBER

BOOKS

DECEMBER

1999 JANUARY

FEBRUARY

MARCH

APRIL

MAY

JUNE

JULY

_____

_____

AUGUST

_____

_____

SEPTEMBER

_____

_____

OCTOBER

_____

_____

NOVEMBER

_____

_____

DECEMBER

_____

_____

1999

MOVIES

BOOKS

2000 JANUARY

FEBRUARY

HEADLINES

MARCH

APRIL

MAY

JUNE

JULY

_____

_____

AUGUST

_____

_____

SEPTEMBER

_____

_____

OCTOBER

_____

_____

NOVEMBER

_____

_____

DECEMBER

_____

_____

_____

2000

SONGS

MOVIES

BOOKS

Whew, We Made It!

THE REST

OF YOUR

LIFELOG

PERSONAL INFORMATION

Birth Time _____ Date _____

Place _____

Who You Are Named After _____

What Your Name Means _____

Circumstances _____

Schools _____

_____

_____

Colleges _____

_____

_____

Training _____

_____

_____

Awards _____

_____

_____

Banks _____

_____

_____

_____

_____

_____

_____

PERSONAL INFORMATION

Social Security Number

1st Job

Drivers License

Passport Number

Doctors

Dentists

Lawyers

NOTES

NOTES

Great Grandchildren

Grandchildren

Children

You

Brothers and Sisters

Nieces and
Nephews

Aunts and Uncles

Cousins

Parents

Grandparents

Great Grandparents

Great Great Grandparents

Great Grandchildren

Grandchildren

Children

Your Spouse

Brothers and Sisters

Nieces and
Nephews

Aunts and Uncles

Cousins

Parents

Grandparents

Great Grandparents

Great Great Grandparents

BIRTHDAYS AND ANNIVERSARYS

JANUARY

1	2	3	4	5	6	7
8	9	10	11	12	13	14
15	16	17	18	19	20	21
22	23	24	25	26	27	28
29	30	31				

FEBRUARY

1	2	3	4	5	6	7
8	9	10	11	12	13	14
15	16	17	18	19	20	21
22	23	24	25	26	27	28
29						

MARCH

1	2	3	4	5	6	7
8	9	10	11	12	13	14
15	16	17	18	19	20	21
22	23	24	25	26	27	28
29	30	31				

APRIL

1	2	3	4	5	6	7
8	9	10	11	12	13	14
15	16	17	18	19	20	21
22	23	24	25	26	27	28
29	30					

MAY

1	2	3	4	5	6	7
8	9	10	11	12	13	14
15	16	17	18	19	20	21
22	23	24	25	26	27	28
29	30	31				

JUNE

1	2	3	4	5	6	7
8	9	10	11	12	13	14
15	16	17	18	19	20	21
22	23	24	25	26	27	28
29	30					

BIRTHDAYS AND ANNIVERSARYS

JULY

1	2	3	4	5	6	7
8	9	10	11	12	13	14
15	16	17	18	19	20	21
22	23	24	25	26	27	28
29	30	31				

AUGUST

1	2	3	4	5	6	7
8	9	10	11	12	13	14
15	16	17	18	19	20	21
22	23	24	25	26	27	28
29	30	31				

SEPTEMBER

1	2	3	4	5	6	7
8	9	10	11	12	13	14
15	16	17	18	19	20	21
22	23	24	25	26	27	28
29	30					

OCTOBER

1	2	3	4	5	6	7
8	9	10	11	12	13	14
15	16	17	18	19	20	21
22	23	24	25	26	27	28
29	30	31				

NOVEMBER

1	2	3	4	5	6	7
8	9	10	11	12	13	14
15	16	17	18	19	20	21
22	23	24	25	26	27	28
29	30					

DECEMBER

1	2	3	4	5	6	7
8	9	10	11	12	13	14
15	16	17	18	19	20	21
22	23	24	25	26	27	28
29	30	31				

20TH CENTURY CALENDAR

TO FIND YOUR DATES

Choose a Year and the following (#) number will indicated the calendar year to use in finding days and dates of that year. Calendars #1-#7 are for regular years and #8-#14 are for leap years that have an extra day in the month of February.

1900 - #2	1920 - #12	1940 - #9	1960 - #13	1980 - #10
1901 - #3	1921 - #7	1941 - #4	1961 - #1	1981 - #5
1902 - #4	1922 - #1	1942 - #5	1962 - #2	1982 - #6
1903 - #5	1923 - #2	1943 - #6	1963 - #3	1983 - #7
1904 - #13	1924 - #10	1944 - #14	1964 - #11	1984 - #8
1905 - #1	1925 - #5	1945 - #2	1965 - #6	1985 - #3
1906 - #2	1926 - #6	1946 - #3	1966 - #7	1986 - #4
1907 - #3	1927 - #7	1947 - #4	1967 - #1	1987 - #5
1908 - #11	1928 - #8	1948 - #12	1968 - #9	1988 - #13
1909 - #6	1929 - #3	1949 - #7	1969 - #4	1989 - #1
1910 - #7	1930 - #4	1950 - #1	1970 - #5	1990 - #2
1911 - #1	1931 - #5	1951 - #2	1971 - #6	1991 - #3
1912 - #9	1932 - #13	1952 - #10	1972 - #14	1992 - #11
1913 - #4	1933 - #1	1953 - #5	1973 - #2	1993 - #6
1914 - #5	1934 - #2	1954 - #6	1974 - #3	1994 - #7
1915 - #6	1935 - #3	1955 - #7	1975 - #4	1995 - #1
1916 - #14	1936 - #11	1956 - #8	1976 - #12	1996 - #9
1917 - #2	1937 - #6	1957 - #3	1977 - #7	1997 - #4
1918 - #3	1938 - #7	1958 - #4	1978 - #1	1998 - #5
1919 - #4	1939 - #1	1959 - #5	1979 - #2	1999 - #6
				2000 - #14

CALENDAR #1

1905 1911 1922 1933 1939
1950 1961 1967 1978 1989
1995

JANUARY
S M T W T F S
. . . 1 2 3 4
5 6 7 8 9 10 11
12 13 14 15 16 17 18
19 20 21 22 23 24 25
26 27 28

FEBRUARY
S M T W T F S
. . . 1 2 3 4
5 6 7 8 9 10 11
12 13 14 15 16 17 18
19 20 21 22 23 24 25
26 27 28

MARCH
S M T W T F S
. . . 1 2 3 4
5 6 7 8 9 10 11
12 13 14 15 16 17 18
19 20 21 22 23 24 25
26 27 28 29 30 31

APRIL
S M T W T F S
. 1
2 3 4 5 6 7 8
9 10 11 12 13 14 15
16 17 18 19 20 21 22
23 24 25 26 27 28 29
30

MAY
S M T W T F S
. 1 2 3 4 5 6
7 8 9 10 11 12 13
14 15 16 17 18 19 20
21 22 23 24 25 26 27
28 29 30 31

JUNE
S M T W T F S
. . . . 1 2 3
4 5 6 7 8 9 10
11 12 13 14 15 16 17
18 19 20 21 22 23 24
25 26 27 28 29 30

JULY
S M T W T F S
. 1
2 3 4 5 6 7 8
9 10 11 12 13 14 15
16 17 18 19 20 21 22
23 24 25 26 27 28 29
30 31

AUGUST
S M T W T F S
. . 1 2 3 4 5
6 7 8 9 10 11 12
13 14 15 16 17 18 19
20 21 22 23 24 25 26
27 28 2930 31

SEPTEMBER
S M T W T F S
. . . . . 1 2
3 4 5 6 7 8 9
10 11 12 13 14 15 16
17 18 19 20 21 22 23
24 25 26 27 28 29 30

OCTOBER
S M T W T F S
1 2 3 4 5 6 7
8 9 10 11 12 13 14
15 16 17 18 19 20 21
22 23 24 25 26 27 28
29 30 31

NOVEMBER
S M T W T F S
. . . 1 2 3 4
5 6 7 8 9 10 11
12 13 14 15 16 17 18
19 20 21 22 23 24 25
26 27 28 29 30

DECEMBER
S M T W T F S
. . . . . 1 2
3 4 5 6 7 8 9
10 11 12 13 14 15 16
17 18 19 20 21 22 23
24 25 26 27 28 29 30
31

CALENDAR #2

1900 1906 1917 1923 1934
1945 1951 1962 1973 1979
1990

JANUARY
S M T W T F S
. 1 2 3 4 5 6
7 8 9 10 11 12 13
14 15 16 17 18 19 20
21 22 23 24 25 26 27
28 29 30 31

FEBRUARY
S M T W T F S
. . . . 1 2 3
4 5 6 7 8 9 10
11 12 13 14 15 16 17
18 19 20 21 22 23 24
25 26 27 28

MARCH
S M T W T F S
. . . . 1 2 3
4 5 6 7 8 9 10
11 12 13 14 15 16 17
18 19 20 21 22 23 24
25 26 27 28 29 30 31

APRIL
S M T W T F S
1 2 3 4 5 6 7
8 9 10 11 12 13 14
15 16 17 18 19 20 21
22 23 24 25 26 27 28
29 30

MAY
S M T W T F S
. . 1 2 3 4 5
6 7 8 9 10 11 12
13 14 15 16 17 18 19
20 21 22 23 24 25 26
27 28 29 30 31

JUNE
S M T W T F S
. . . . . 1 2
3 4 5 6 7 8 9
10 11 12 13 14 15 16
17 18 19 20 21 22 23
24 25 26 27 28 29 30

JULY
S M T W T F S
1 2 3 4 5 6 7
8 9 10 11 12 13 14
15 16 17 18 19 20 21
22 23 24 25 26 27 28
29 30 31

AUGUST
S M T W T F S
. . . 1 2 3 4
5 6 7 8 9 10 11
12 13 14 15 16 17 18
19 20 21 22 23 24 25
26 27 28 29 30 31

SEPTEMBER
S M T W T F S
. 1
2 3 4 5 6 7 8
9 10 11 12 13 14 15
16 17 18 19 20 21 22
23 24 25 26 27 28 29
30

OCTOBER
S M T W T F S
. 1 2 3 4 5 6
7 8 9 10 11 12 13
14 15 16 17 18 19 20
21 22 23 24 25 26 27
28 29 30 31

NOVEMBER
S M T W T F S
. . . . 1 2 3
4 5 6 7 8 9 10
11 12 13 14 15 16 17
18 19 20 21 22 23 24
25 26 27 28 29 30

DECEMBER
S M T W T F S
. 1
2 3 4 5 6 7 8
9 10 11 12 13 14 15
16 17 18 19 20 21 22
23 24 25 26 27 28 29
30 31

CALENDAR #3

1901 1907 1918 1929 1935
1946 1957 1963 1974 1985
1991

JANUARY
S M T W T F S
. . 1 2 3 4 5
6 7 8 9 10 11 12
13 14 15 16 17 18 19
20 21 22 23 24 25 26
27 28 29 30 31

FEBRUARY
S M T W T F S
. . . . . 1 2
3 4 5 6 7 8 9
10 11 12 13 14 15 16
17 18 19 20 21 22 23
24 25 26 27 28

MARCH
S M T W T F S
. . . . . 1 2
3 4 5 6 7 8 9
10 11 12 13 14 15 16
17 18 19 20 21 22 23
24 25 26 27 28 29 30
31

APRIL
S M T W T F S
. 1 2 3 4 5 6
7 8 9 10 11 12 13
14 15 16 17 18 19 20
21 22 23 24 25 26 27
28 29 30

MAY
S M T W T F S
. . . 1 2 3 4
5 6 7 8 9 10 11
12 13 14 15 16 17 18
19 20 21 22 23 24 25
26 27 28 29 30 31

JUNE
S M T W T F S
. 1
2 3 4 5 6 7 8
9 10 11 12 13 14 15
16 17 18 19 20 21 22
23 24 25 26 27 28 29
30

JULY
S M T W T F S
. 1 2 3 4 5 6
7 8 9 10 11 12 13
14 15 16 17 18 19 20
21 22 23 24 25 26 27
28 29 30 31

AUGUST
S M T W T F S
. . . . 1 2 3
4 5 6 7 8 9 10
11 12 13 14 15 16 17
18 19 20 21 22 23 24
25 26 27 28 29 30 31

SEPTEMBER
S M T W T F S
1 2 3 4 5 6 7
8 9 10 11 12 13 14
15 16 17 18 19 20 21
22 23 24 25 26 27 28
29 30

OCTOBER
S M T W T F S
. . 1 2 3 4 5
6 7 8 9 10 11 12
13 14 15 16 17 18 19
20 21 22 23 24 25 26
27 28 29 30 31

NOVEMBER
S M T W T F S
. . . . . 1 2
3 4 5 6 7 8 9
10 11 12 13 14 15 16
17 18 19 20 21 22 23
24 25 26 27 28 29 30

DECEMBER
S M T W T F S
1 2 3 4 5 6 7
8 9 10 11 12 13 14
15 16 17 18 19 20 21
22 23 24 25 26 27 28
29 30 31

CALENDAR # 4

1902   1913   1919   1930   1941
1947   1958   1969   1975   1986
1997

```
       JANUARY                FEBRUARY                 MARCH
 S  M  T  W  T  F  S     S  M  T  W  T  F  S     S  M  T  W  T  F  S
          1  2  3  4                       1                       1
 5  6  7  8  9 10 11     2  3  4  5  6  7  8     2  3  4  5  6  7  8
12 13 14 15 16 17 18     9 10 11 12 13 14 15     9 10 11 12 13 14 15
19 20 21 22 23 24 25    16 17 18 19 20 21 22    16 17 18 19 20 21 22
26 27 28 29 30 31       23 24 25 26 27 28       23 24 25 26 27 28 29
                                                30 31

        APRIL                    MAY                     JUNB
 S  M  T  W  T  F  S     S  M  T  W  T  F  S     S  M  T  W  T  F  S
          1  2  3  4                       1     1  2  3  4  5  6  7
 6  7  8  9 10 11 12     4  5  6  7  8  9 10     8  9 10 11 12 13 14
13 14 15 16 17 18 19    11 12 13 14 15 16 17    15 16 17 18 19 20 21
20 21 22 23 24 25 26    18 19 20 21 22 23 24    22 23 24 25 26 27 28
27 28 29 30             25 26 27 28 29 30 31    29 30

         JULY                  AUGUST                 SEPTEMBER
 S  M  T  W  T  F  S     S  M  T  W  T  F  S     S  M  T  W  T  F  S
          1  2  3  4  5                 1  2              1  2  3  4  5  6
 6  7  8  9 10 11 12     3  4  5  6  7  8  9     7  8  9 10 11 12 13
13 14 15 16 17 18 19    10 11 12 13 14 15 16    14 15 16 17 18 19 20
20 21 22 23 24 25 26    17 18 19 20 21 22 23    21 22 23 24 25 26 27
27 28 29 30 31          24 25 26 27 28 29 30    28 29 30
                        31

       OCTOBER                NOVEMBER                DECEMBER
 S  M  T  W  T  F  S     S  M  T  W  T  F  S     S  M  T  W  T  F  S
             1  2  3  4                       1              1  2  3  4  5  6
 5  6  7  8  9 10 11     2  3  4  5  6  7  8     7  8  9 10 11 12 13
12 13 14 15 16 17 18     9 10 11 12 13 14 15    14 15 16 17 18 19 20
19 20 21 22 23 24 25    16 17 18 19 20 21 22    21 22 23 24 25 26 27
26 27 28 29 30 31       23 24 25 26 27 28 29    28 29 30 31
                        30
```

CALENDAR #5

1903   1914   1925   1931   1942
1953   1959   1970   1981   1987
1998

```
       JANUARY                FEBRUARY                 MARCH
 S  M  T  W  T  F  S     S  M  T  W  T  F  S     S  M  T  W  T  F  S
             1  2  3     1  2  3  4  5  6  7     1  2  3  4  5  6  7
 4  5  6  7  8  9 10     8  9 10 11 12 13 14     8  9 10 11 12 13 14
11 12 13 14 15 16 17    15 16 17 18 19 20 21    15 16 17 18 19 20 21
18 19 20 21 22 23 24    22 23 24 25 26 27 28    22 23 24 25 26 27 28
25 26 27 28 29 30 31                            29 30 31

        APRIL                    MAY                     JUNE
 S  M  T  W  T  F  S     S  M  T  W  T  F  S     S  M  T  W  T  F  S
          1  2  3  4                    1  2        1  2  3  4  5  6
 5  6  7  8  9 10 11     3  4  5  6  7  8  9     7  8  9 10 11 12 13
12 13 14 15 16 17 18    10 11 12 13 14 15 16    14 15 16 17 18 19 20
19 20 21 22 23 24 25    17 18 19 20 21 22 23    21 22 23 24 25 26 27
26 27 28 29 30          24 25 26 27 28 29 30    28 29 30
                        31

         JULY                  AUGUST                 SEPTEMBER
 S  M  T  W  T  F  S     S  M  T  W  T  F  S     S  M  T  W  T  F  S
          1  2  3  4                       1              1  2  3  4  5
 5  6  7  8  9 10 11     2  3  4  5  6  7  8     6  7  8  9 10 11 12
12 13 14 15 16 17 18     9 10 11 12 13 14 15    13 14 15 16 17 18 19
19 20 21 22 23 24 25    16 17 18 19 20 21 22    20 21 22 23 24 25 26
26 27 28 29 30 31       23 24 25 26 27 28 29    27 28 29 30
                        30 31

       OCTOBER                NOVEMBER                DECEMBER
 S  M  T  W  T  F  S     S  M  T  W  T  F  S     S  M  T  W  T  F  S
             1  2  3     1  2  3  4  5  6  7              1  2  3  4  5
 4  5  6  7  8  9 10     8  9 10 11 12 13 14     6  7  8  9 10 11 12
11 12 13 14 15 16 17    15 16 17 18 19 20 21    13 14 15 16 17 18 19
18 19 20 21 22 23 24    22 23 24 25 26 27 28    20 21 22 23 24 25 26
25 26 27 28 29 30 31    29 30                   27 28 29 30 31
```

CALENDAR #6

1909   1915   1926   1937   1943
1954   1965   1971   1982   1993
1999

```
       JANUARY                FEBRUARY                 MARCH
 S  M  T  W  T  F  S     S  M  T  W  T  F  S     S  M  T  W  T  F  S
                1  2              1  2  3  4  5  6              1  2  3  4  5  6
 3  4  5  6  7  8  9     7  8  9 10 11 12 13     7  8  9 10 11 12 13
10 11 12 13 14 15 16    14 15 16 17 18 19 20    14 15 16 17 18 19 20
17 18 19 20 21 22 23    21 22 23 24 25 26 27    21 22 23 24 25 26 27
24 25 26 27 28 29 30    28                      28 29 30 31
31

        APRIL                    MAY                     JUNE
 S  M  T  W  T  F  S     S  M  T  W  T  F  S     S  M  T  W  T  F  S
          1  2  3                          1              1  2  3  4  5
 4  5  6  7  8  9 10     2  3  4  5  6  7  8     6  7  8  9 10 11 12
11 12 13 14 15 16 17     9 10 11 12 13 14 15    13 14 15 16 17 18 19
18 19 20 21 22 23 24    16 17 18 19 20 21 22    20 21 22 23 24 25 26
25 26 27 28 29 30       23 24 25 26 27 28 29    27 28 29
                        30 31

         JULY                  AUGUST                 SEPTEMBER
 S  M  T  W  T  F  S     S  M  T  W  T  F  S     S  M  T  W  T  F  S
             1  2  3     1  2  3  4  5  6  7                    1  2  3  4
 4  5  6  7  8  9 10     8  9 10 11 12 13 14     5  6  7  8  9 10 11
11 12 13 14 15 16 17    15 16 17 18 19 20 21    12 13 14 15 16 17 18
18 19 20 21 22 23 24    22 23 24 25 26 27 28    19 20 21 22 23 24 25
25 26 27 28 29 30 31    29 30 31                26 27 28 29 30

       OCTOBER                NOVEMBER                DECEMBER
 S  M  T  W  T  F  S     S  M  T  W  T  F  S     S  M  T  W  T  F  S
                1  2              1  2  3  4  5  6              1  2  3  4
 3  4  5  6  7  8  9     7  8  9 10 11 12 13     5  6  7  8  9 10 11
10 11 12 13 14 15 16    14 15 16 17 18 19 20    12 13 14 15 16 17 18
17 18 19 20 21 22 23    21 22 23 24 25 26 27    19 20 21 22 23 24 25
24 25 26 27 28 29 30    28 29 30                26 27 28 29 30 31
31
```

CALENDAR #7

1910   1921   1927   1938   1949
1955   1966   1977   1983   1994

```
       JANUARY                FEBRUARY                 MARCH
 S  M  T  W  T  F  S     S  M  T  W  T  F  S     S  M  T  W  T  F  S
                   1              1  2  3  4  5              1  2  3  4  5
 2  3  4  5  6  7  8     6  7  8  9 10 11 12     6  7  8  9 10 11 12
 9 10 11 12 13 14 15    13 14 15 16 17 18 19    13 14 15 16 17 18 19
16 17 18 19 20 21 22    20 21 22 23 24 25 26    20 21 22 23 24 25 26
23 24 25 26 27 28 29    27 28                   27 28 29 30 31
30 31

        APRIL                    MAY                     JUNE
 S  M  T  W  T  F  S     S  M  T  W  T  F  S     S  M  T  W  T  F  S
                1  2     1  2  3  4  5  6  7                 1  2  3  4
 3  4  5  6  7  8  9     8  9 10 11 12 13 14     5  6  7  8  9 10 11
10 11 12 13 14 15 16    15 16 17 18 19 20 21    12 13 14 15 16 17 18
17 18 19 20 21 22 23    22 23 24 25 26 27 28    19 20 21 22 23 24 25
24 25 26 27 28 29 30    29 30 31                26 27 28 29 30

         JULY                  AUGUST                 SEPTEMBER
 S  M  T  W  T  F  S     S  M  T  W  T  F  S     S  M  T  W  T  F  S
                1  2     1  2  3  4  5  6                       1  2  3
 3  4  5  6  7  8  9     7  8  9 10 11 12 13     4  5  6  7  8  9 10
10 11 12 13 14 15 16    14 15 16 17 18 19 20    11 12 13 14 15 16 17
17 18 19 20 21 22 23    21 22 23 24 25 26 27    18 19 20 21 22 23 24
24 25 26 27 28 29 30    28 29 30 31             25 26 27 28 29 30
31

       OCTOBER                NOVEMBER                DECEMBER
 S  M  T  W  T  F  S     S  M  T  W  T  F  S     S  M  T  W  T  F  S
                   1              1  2  3  4  5              1  2  3
 2  3  4  5  6  7  8     6  7  8  9 10 11 12     4  5  6  7  8  9 10
 9 10 11 12 13 14 15    13 14 15 16 17 18 19    11 12 13 14 15 16 17
16 17 18 19 20 21 22    20 21 22 23 24 25 26    18 19 20 21 22 23 24
23 24 25 26 27 28 29    27 28 29 30             25 26 27 28 29 30 31
30 31
```

20TH CENTURY CALENDAR

TO FIND YOUR DATES

Choose Year and the following (#) number will indicated the calendar year to use in finding days and dates of that year. Calendars #1-#7 are for regular years and #8-#14 are for leap years that have an extra day in the month of February.

1900 - #2	1920 - #12	1940 - #9	1960 - #13	1980 - #10
1901 - #3	1921 - #7	1941 - #4	1961 - #1	1981 - #5
1902 - #4	1922 - #1	1942 - #5	1962 - #2	1982 - #6
1903 - #5	1923 - #2	1943 - #6	1963 - #3	1983 - #7
1904 - #13	1924 - #10	1944 - #14	1964 - #11	1984 - #8
1905 - #1	1925 - #5	1945 - #2	1965 - #6	1985 - #3
1906 - #2	1926 - #6	1946 - #3	1966 - #7	1986 - #4
1907 - #3	1927 - #7	1947 - #4	1967 - #1	1987 - #5
1908 - #11	1928 - #8	1948 - #12	1968 - #9	1988 - #13
1909 - #6	1929 - #3	1949 - #7	1969 - #4	1989 - #1
1910 - #7	1930 - #4	1950 - #1	1970 - #5	1990 - #2
1911 - #1	1931 - #5	1951 - #2	1971 - #6	1991 - #3
1912 - #9	1932 - #13	1952 - #10	1972 - #14	1992 - #11
1913 - #4	1933 - #1	1953 - #5	1973 - #2	1993 - #6
1914 - #5	1934 - #2	1954 - #6	1974 - #3	1994 - #7
1915 - #6	1935 - #3	1955 - #7	1975 - #4	1995 - #1
1916 - #14	1936 - #11	1956 - #8	1976 - #12	1996 - #9
1917 - #2	1937 - #6	1957 - #3	1977 - #7	1997 - #4
1918 - #3	1938 - #7	1958 - #4	1978 - #1	1998 - #5
1919 - #4	1939 - #1	1959 - #5	1979 - #2	1999 - #6
				2000 - #14

CALENDAR #8

1928   1956   1984

JANUARY
```
S  M  T  W  T  F  S
1  2  3  4  5  6  7
8  9 10 11 12 13 14
15 16 17 18 19 20 21
22 23 24 25 26 27 28
29 30 31
```

FEBRUARY
```
S  M  T  W  T  F  S
            1  2  3  4
5  6  7  8  9 10 11
12 13 14 15 16 17 18
19 20 21 22 23 24 25
26 27 28 29
```

MARCH
```
S  M  T  W  T  F  S
               1  2  3
4  5  6  7  8  9 10
11 12 13 14 15 16 17
18 19 20 21 22 23 24
25 26 27 28 29 30 31
```

APRIL
```
S  M  T  W  T  F  S
1  2  3  4  5  6  7
8  9 10 11 12 13 14
15 16 17 18 19 20 21
22 23 24 25 26 27 28
29 30
```

MAY
```
S  M  T  W  T  F  S
      1  2  3  4  5
6  7  8  9 10 11 12
13 14 15 16 17 18 19
20 21 22 23 24 25 26
27 28 29 30 31
```

JUNE
```
S  M  T  W  T  F  S
                  1  2
3  4  5  6  7  8  9
10 11 12 13 14 15 16
17 18 19 20 21 22 23
24 25 26 27 28 29 30
```

JULY
```
S  M  T  W  T  F  S
1  2  3  4  5  6  7
8  9 10 11 12 13 14
15 16 17 18 19 20 21
22 23 24 25 26 27 28
29 30 31
```

AUGUST
```
S  M  T  W  T  F  S
         1  2  3  4
5  6  7  8  9 10 11
12 13 14 15 16 17 18
19 20 21 22 23 24 25
26 27 28 29 30 31
```

SEPTEMBER
```
S  M  T  W  T  F  S
                     1
2  3  4  5  6  7  8
9 10 11 12 13 14 15
16 17 18 19 20 21 22
23 24 25 26 27 28 29
30
```

OCTOBER
```
S  M  T  W  T  F  S
      1  2  3  4  5  6
7  8  9 10 11 12 13
14 15 16 17 18 19 20
21 22 23 24 25 26 27
28 29 30 31
```

NOVEMBER
```
S  M  T  W  T  F  S
            1  2  3
4  5  6  7  8  9 10
11 12 13 14 15 16 17
18 19 20 21 22 23 24
25 16 27 28 29 30
```

DECEMBER
```
S  M  T  W  T  F  S
                     1
2  3  4  5  6  7  8
9 10 11 12 13 14 15
16 17 18 19 20 21 22
23 24 25 26 27 28 29
30 31
```

CALENDAR #9

1912   1940   1968   1996

JANUARY
```
S  M  T  W  T  F  S
1  2  3  4  5  6
7  8  9 10 11 12 13
14 15 16 17 18 19 20
21 22 23 24 25 26 27
28 29 30 31
```

FEBRUARY
```
S  M  T  W  T  F  S
               1  2  3
4  5  6  7  8  9 10
11 12 13 14 15 16 17
18 19 20 21 22 23 24
25 26 27 28 29
```

MARCH
```
S  M  T  W  T  F  S
                  1  2
3  4  5  6  7  8  9
10 11 12 13 14 15 16
17 18 19 20 21 22 23
24 25 26 27 28 29 30
31
```

APRIL
```
S  M  T  W  T  F  S
1  2  3  4  5  6
7  8  9 10 11 12 13
14 15 16 17 18 19 20
21 22 23 24 25 26 27
28 29 30
```

MAY
```
S  M  T  W  T  F  S
         1  2  3  4
5  6  7  8  9 10 11
12 13 14 15 16 17 18
19 20 21 22 23 24 25
26 27 28 29 30 31
```

JUNE
```
S  M  T  W  T  F  S
                     1
2  3  4  5  6  7  8
9 10 11 12 13 14 15
16 17 18 19 20 21 22
23 24 25 26 27 28 29
30
```

JULY
```
S  M  T  W  T  F  S
1  2  3  4  5  6
7  8  9 10 11 12 13
14 15 16 17 18 19 20
21 22 23 24 25 26 27
28 29 30 31
```

AUGUST
```
S  M  T  W  T  F  S
            1  2  3
4  5  6  7  8  9 10
11 12 13 14 15 16 17
18 19 20 21 22 23 24
25 26 27 28 29 30 31
```

SEPTEMBER
```
S  M  T  W  T  F  S
1  2  3  4  5  6  7
8  9 10 11 12 13 14
15 16 17 18 19 20 21
22 23 24 25 26 27 28
29 30
```

OCTOBER
```
S  M  T  W  T  F  S
      1  2  3  4  5
6  7  8  9 10 11 12
13 14 15 16 17 18 19
20 21 22 23 24 25 26
27 28 29 30 31
```

NOVEMBER
```
S  M  T  W  T  F  S
                  1  2
3  4  5  6  7  8  9
10 11 12 13 14 15 16
17 18 19 20 21 22 23
24 25 26 27 28 29 30
```

DECEMBER
```
S  M  T  W  T  F  S
1  2  3  4  5  6  7
8  9 10 11 12 13 14
15 16 17 18 19 20 21
22 23 24 25 26 27 28
29 30 31
```

CALENDAR #10

1924   1952   1980

JANUARY
```
S  M  T  W  T  F  S
      1  2  3  4  5
6  7  8  9 10 11 12
13 14 15 16 17 18 19
20 21 22 23 24 25 26
27 28 29 30 31
```

FEBRUARY
```
S  M  T  W  T  F  S
                  1  2
3  4  5  6  7  8  9
10 11 12 13 14 15 16
17 18 19 20 21 22 23
24 25 26 27 28 29
```

MARCH
```
S  M  T  W  T  F  S
                     1
2  3  4  5  6  7  8
9 10 11 12 13 14 15
16 17 18 19 20 21 22
23 24 25 26 27 28 29
30 31
```

APRIL
```
S  M  T  W  T  F  S
      1  2  3  4  5
6  7  8  9 10 11 12
13 14 15 16 17 18 19
20 21 22 23 24 25 26
27 28 29 30
```

MAY
```
S  M  T  W  T  F  S
               1  2  3
4  5  6  7  8  9 10
11 12 13 14 15 16 17
18 19 20 21 22 23 24
25 26 27 28 29 30 31
```

JUNE
```
S  M  T  W  T  F  S
1  2  3  4  5  6  7
8  9 10 11 12 13 14
15 16 17 18 19 20 21
22 23 24 25 26 27 28
29 30
```

JULY
```
S  M  T  W  T  F  S
      1  2  3  4  5
6  7  8  9 10 11 12
13 14 15 16 17 18 19
20 21 22 23 24 25 26
27 28 29 30 31
```

AUGUST
```
S  M  T  W  T  F  S
                  1  2
3  4  5  6  7  8  9
10 11 12 13 14 15 16
17 18 19 20 21 22 23
24 25 26 27 28 29 30
31
```

SEPTEMBER
```
S  M  T  W  T  F  S
   1  2  3  4  5  6
7  8  9 10 11 12 13
14 15 16 17 18 19 20
21 22 23 24 25 26 27
28 29 30
```

OCTOBER
```
S  M  T  W  T  F  S
               1  2  3
5  6  7  8  9 10 11
12 13 14 15 16 17 18
19 20 21 22 23 24 25
26 27 28 29 30 31
```

NOVEMBER
```
S  M  T  W  T  F  S
                  1
2  3  4  5  6  7  8
9 10 11 12 13 14 15
16 17 18 19 20 21 22
23 24 25 26 27 28 29
30
```

DECEMBER
```
S  M  T  W  T  F  S
   1  2  3  4  5  6
7  8  9 10 11 12 13
14 15 16 17 18 19 20
21 22 23 24 25 26 27
28 29 30 31
```

20TH CENTURY CALENDAR

CALENDAR # 11

1908   1936   1964   1992

JANUARY
S M T W T F S
         1 2 3 4
5 6 7 8 9 10 11
12 13 14 15 16 17 18
19 20 21 22 23 24 25
26 27 28 29 30 31

FEBRUARY
S M T W T F S
                     1
2 3 4 5 6 7 8
9 10 11 12 13 14 15
16 17 18 19 20 21 22
23 24 25 26 27 28 29

MARCH
S M T W T F S
1 2 3 4 5 6 7
8 9 10 11 12 13 14
15 16 17 18 19 20 21
22 23 24 25 26 27 28
29 30 31

APRIL
S M T W T F S
            1 2 3 4
5 6 7 8 9 10 11
12 13 14 15 16 17 18
19 20 21 22 23 24 25
26 27 28 29 30

MAY
S M T W T F S
                  1 2
3 4 5 6 7 8 9
10 11 12 13 14 15 16
17 18 19 20 21 22 23
24 25 26 27 28 29 30
31

JUNE
S M T W T F S
      1 2 3 4 5 6
7 8 9 10 11 12 13
14 15 16 17 18 19 20
21 22 23 24 25 26 27
28 29 30

JULY
S M T W T F S
            1 2 3 4
5 6 7 8 9 10 11
12 13 14 15 16 17 18
19 20 21 22 23 24 25
26 27 28 29 30 31

AUGUST
S M T W T F S
                     1
2 3 4 5 6 7 8
9 10 11 12 13 14 15
16 17 18 19 20 21 22
23 24 25 26 27 28 29
30 31

SEPTEMBER
S M T W T F S
         1 2 3 4 5
6 7 8 9 10 11 12
13 14 15 16 17 18 19
20 21 22 23 24 25 26
27 28 29 30

OCTOBER
S M T W T F S
               1 2 3
4 5 6 7 8 9 10
11 12 13 14 15 16 17
18 19 20 21 22 23 24
25 26 27 28 29 30 31

NOVEMBER
S M T W T F S
1 2 3 4 5 6 7
8 9 10 11 12 13 14
15 16 17 18 19 20 21
22 23 24 25 26 27 28
29 30

DECEMBER
S M T W T F S
         1 2 3 4 5
6 7 8 9 10 11 12
13 14 15 16 17 18 19
20 21 22 23 24 25 26
27 28 29 30 31

CALENDAR # 12

1920   1948   1976

JANUARY
S M T W T F S
               1 2 3
4 5 6 7 8 9 10
11 12 13 14 15 16 17
18 19 20 21 22 23 24
25 26 27 28 29 30 31

FEBRUARY
S M T W T F S
1 2 3 4 5 6 7
8 9 10 11 12 13 14
15 16 17 18 19 20 21
22 23 24 25 26 27 28
29

MARCH
S M T W T F S
1 2 3 4 5 6
7 8 9 10 11 12 13
14 15 16 17 18 19 20
21 22 23 24 25 26 27
28 29 30 31

APRIL
S M T W T F S
               1 2 3
4 5 6 7 8 9 10
11 12 13 14 15 16 17
18 19 20 21 22 23 24
25 26 27 28 29 30

MAY
S M T W T F S
                     1
2 3 4 5 6 7 8
9 10 11 12 13 14 15
16 17 18 19 20 21 22
23 24 25 26 27 28 29
30 31

JUNE
S M T W T F S
         1 2 3 4 5
6 7 8 9 10 11 12
13 14 15 16 17 18 19
20 21 22 23 24 25 26
27 28 29 30

JULY
S M T W T F S
               1 2 3
4 5 6 7 8 9 10
11 12 13 14 15 16 17
18 19 20 21 22 23 24
25 26 27 28 29 30 31

AUGUST
S M T W T F S
1 2 3 4 5 6 7
8 9 10 11 12 13 14
15 16 17 18 19 20 21
22 23 24 25 26 27 28
29 30 31

SEPTEMBER
S M T W T F S
            1 2 3 4
5 6 7 8 9 10 11
12 13 14 15 16 17 18
19 20 21 22 23 24 25
26 27 28 29 30

OCTOBER
S M T W T F S
                  1 2
3 4 5 6 7 8 9
10 11 12 13 14 15 16
17 18 19 20 21 22 23
24 25 26 27 28 29 30
31

NOVEMBER
S M T W T F S
      1 2 3 4 5 6
7 8 9 10 11 12 13
14 15 16 17 18 19 20
21 22 23 24 25 26 27
28 29 30

DECEMBER
S M T W T F S
            1 2 3 4
5 6 7 8 9 10 11
12 13 14 15 16 17 18
19 20 21 22 23 24 25
26 27 28 29 30 31

CALENDAR # 13

1904   1932   1960   1988

JANUARY
S M T W T F S
                  1 2
3 4 5 6 7 8 9
10 11 12 13 14 15 16
17 18 19 20 21 22 23
24 25 26 27 28 29 30
31

FEBRUARY
S M T W T F S
      1 2 3 4 5 6
7 8 9 10 11 12 13
14 15 16 17 18 19 20
21 22 23 24 25 26 27
28 29

MARCH
S M T W T F S
         1 2 3 4 5
6 7 8 9 10 11 12
13 14 15 16 17 18 19
20 21 22 23 24 25 26
27 28 29 30 31

APRIL
S M T W T F S
                  1 2
3 4 5 6 7 8 9
10 11 12 13 14 15 16
17 18 19 20 21 22 23
24 25 26 27 28 29 30

MAY
S M T W T F S
1 2 3 4 5 6 7
8 9 10 11 12 13 14
15 16 17 18 19 20 21
22 23 24 25 26 27 28
29 30 31

JUNE
S M T W T F S
            1 2 3 4
5 6 7 8 9 10 11
12 13 14 15 16 17 18
19 20 21 22 23 24 25
26 27 28 29 30

JULY
S M T W T F S
                  1 2
3 4 5 6 7 8 9
10 11 12 13 14 15 16
17 18 19 20 21 22 23
24 25 26 27 28 29 30
31

AUGUST
S M T W T F S
      1 2 3 4 5 6
7 8 9 10 11 12 13
14 15 16 17 18 19 20
21 22 23 24 25 26 27
28 29 30 31

SEPTEMBER
S M T W T F S
                1 2 3
4 5 6 7 8 9 10
11 12 13 14 15 16 17
18 19 20 21 22 23 24
25 26 27 28 29 30

OCTOBER
S M T W T F S
                     1
2 3 4 5 6 7 8
9 10 11 12 13 14 15
16 17 18 19 20 21 22
23 24 25 26 27 28 29
30 31

NOVEMBER
S M T W T F S
         1 2 3 4 5
6 7 8 9 10 11 12
13 14 15 16 17 18 19
20 21 22 23 24 25 26
27 28 29 30

DECEMBER
S M T W T F S
               1 2 3
4 5 6 7 8 9 10
11 12 13 14 15 16 17
18 19 20 21 22 23 24
25 26 27 28 29 30 31

CALENDAR # 14

1916   1944   1972   2000

JANUARY
S M T W T F S
                     1
2 3 4 5 6 7 8
9 10 11 12 13 14 15
16 17 18 19 20 21 22
23 24 25 26 27 28 29
30 31

FEBRUARY
S M T W T F S
         1 2 3 4 5
6 7 8 9 10 11 12
13 14 15 16 17 18 19
20 21 22 23 24 25 26
27 28 29

MARCH
S M T W T F S
               1 2 3 4
5 6 7 8 9 10 11
12 13 14 15 16 17 18
19 20 21 22 23 24 25
26 27 28 29 30 31

APRIL
S M T W T F S
                     1
2 3 4 5 6 7 8
9 10 11 12 13 14 15
16 17 18 19 20 21 22
23 24 25 26 27 28 29
30

MAY
S M T W T F S
      1 2 3 4 5 6
7 8 9 10 11 12 13
14 15 16 17 18 19 20
21 22 23 24 25 26 27
28 29 30 31

JUNE
S M T W T F S
                  1 2 3
4 5 6 7 8 9 10
11 12 13 14 15 16 17
18 19 20 21 22 23 24
25 26 27 28 29 30

JULY
S M T W T F S
                     1
2 3 4 5 6 7 8
9 10 11 12 13 14 15
16 17 18 19 20 21 22
23 24 25 26 27 28 29
30 31

AUGUST
S M T W T F S
            1 2 3 4 5
6 7 8 9 10 11 12
13 14 15 16 17 18 19
20 21 22 23 24 25 26
27 28 29 30 31

SEPTEMBER
S M T W T F S
                     1 2
3 4 5 6 7 8 9
10 11 12 13 14 15 16
17 18 19 20 21 22 23
24 25 26 27 28 29 30

OCTOBER
S M T W T F S
1 2 3 4 5 6 7
8 9 10 11 12 13 14
15 16 17 18 19 20 21
22 23 24 25 26 27 28
29 30 31

NOVEMBER
S M T W T F S
            1 2 3 4
5 6 7 8 9 10 11
12 13 14 15 16 17 18
19 20 21 22 23 24 25
26 27 28 29 30

DECEMBER
S M T W T F S
                  1 2
3 4 5 6 7 8 9
10 11 12 13 14 15 16
17 18 19 20 21 22 23
24 25 26 27 28 29 30
31

PERSONAL
CHRONOLOGY

1900

President William McKinley · American Baseball League · Carrie Nation

Family _____ Friends _____

Homes _____ Pets _____ Cars _____

Jobs _____ Education _____

Medical History _____

1901

Presidents William McKinley and Theodore Roosevelt · Assassination

Family _____ Friends _____

Homes _____ Pets _____ Cars _____

Jobs _____ Education _____

Medical History _____

1902

President Theodore Roosevelt · Rose Bowl · Teddy Bears · Gibson Girls

Family _____ Friends _____

Homes _____ Pets _____ Cars _____

Jobs _____ Education _____

Medical History _____

1903

President Theodore Roosevelt · Wright Brothers Fly at Kitty Hawk

Family _____ Friends _____

Homes _____ Pets _____ Cars _____

Jobs _____ Education _____

Medical History _____

1904

President Theodore Roosevelt · St Louis Exposition · 1st Cadillac

Family _____ Friends _____

Homes _____ Pets _____ Cars _____

Jobs _____ Education _____

Medical History _____

PERSONAL CHRONOLOGY

President Theodore Roosevelt · Einstein Proposes E=MC^2

1905

Family   Friends

Homes   Pets   Cars

Jobs   Education

Medical History

President Theodore Roosevelt · San Francisco Earthquake and Fire

1906

Family   Friends

Homes   Pets   Cars

Jobs   Education

Medical History

President Theodore Roosevelt · Oklahoma Becomes a State

1907

Family   Friends

Homes   Pets   Cars

Jobs   Education

Medical History

President Theodore Roosevelt · Henry Ford Offers Model-T Ford, $850

1908

Family   Friends

Homes   Pets   Cars

Jobs   Education

Medical History

President William H Taft · Admiral Peary Reaches the North Pole

1909

Family   Friends

Homes   Pets   Cars

Jobs   Education

Medical History

1910

President William H Taft · Halley's Comet · Boy Scouts · Campfire Girls

Family   Friends

Homes   Pets   Cars

Jobs   Education

Medical History

1911

President William H Taft · Pulitzer Prizes · Mexican Revolution

Family   Friends

Homes   Pets   Cars

Jobs   Education

Medical History

1912

President Woodrow Wilson · Titanic Sinks · US Marines Go to Cuba

Family   Friends

Homes   Pets   Cars

Jobs   Education

Medical History

1913

President Woodrow Wilson · Income Tax · Panama Canal Opens

Family   Friends

Homes   Pets   Cars

Jobs   Education

Medical History

1914

President Woodrow Wilson · 1st Mother's Day · World War I

Family   Friends

Homes   Pets   Cars

Jobs   Education

Medical History

PERSONAL CHRONOLOGY

President Woodrow Wilson • World War I • Mata Hari • *Lusitania*

1915

Family	Friends

Homes	Pets	Cars

Jobs	Education

Medical History

President Woodrow Wilson • Pancho Villa • Virgin Islands • Mercury Dime

1916

Family	Friends

Homes	Pets	Cars

Jobs	Education

Medical History

President Woodrow Wilson • US Enters World War I • General Pershing

1917

Family	Friends

Homes	Pets	Cars

Jobs	Education

Medical History

President Woodrow Wilson • World War I Ends • Jazz Age

1918

Family	Friends

Homes	Pets	Cars

Jobs	Education

Medical History

President Woodrow Wilson • Treaty of Versailles • League of Nations

1919

Family	Friends

Homes	Pets	Cars

Jobs	Education

Medical History

1920

President Warren G Harding • Prohibition • Women Vote • Black Sox

Family   Friends

Homes   Pets   Cars

Jobs   Education

Medical History

1921

President Warren G Harding • Insulin • Valentino • Mary Pickford

Family   Friends

Homes   Pets   Cars

Jobs   Education

Medical History

1922

President Warren G Harding • Radio • Teapot Dome Scandal

Family   Friends

Homes   Pets   Cars

Jobs   Education

Medical History

1923

Presidents Warren G Harding and Calvin Coolidge • Vaudeville

Family   Friends

Homes   Pets   Cars

Jobs   Education

Medical History

1924

President Calvin Coolidge • 1st Winter Olympic Games

Family   Friends

Homes   Pets   Cars

Jobs   Education

Medical History

PERSONAL CHRONOLOGY

President Calvin Coolidge · Chaplin, Disney, Valentino, Fairbanks, Gish

1925

Family   Friends

Homes   Pets   Cars

Jobs   Education

Medical History

President Calvin Coolidge · Gertrude Ederle · Stanlin · Speed of Light

1926

Family   Friends

Homes   Pets   Cars

Jobs   Education

Medical History

President Calvin Coolidge · Lindbergh · Babe Ruth 60 Home Runs

1927

Family   Friends

Homes   Pets   Cars

Jobs   Education

Medical History

President Calvin Coolidge · Mickey Mouse · Penicillin · Mt Palomar

1928

Family   Friends

Homes   Pets   Cars

Jobs   Education

Medical History

President Herbert Hoover · Stock Market Crash · The Goldbergs on Radio

1929

Family   Friends

Homes   Pets   Cars

Jobs   Education

Medical History

1930

President Herbert Hoover · Depression · Pluto · American Gothic

Family _____ Friends _____

Homes _____ Pets _____ Cars _____

Jobs _____ Education _____

Medical History _____

1931

President Herbert Hoover · Empire State Building · Star-Spangled Banner

Family _____ Friends _____

Homes _____ Pets _____ Cars _____

Jobs _____ Education _____

Medical History _____

1932

President Franklin D Roosevelt · Lindbergh Baby · Al Capone Goes to Jail

Family _____ Friends _____

Homes _____ Pets _____ Cars _____

Jobs _____ Education _____

Medical History _____

1933

President Franklin D Roosevelt · Prohibition Ends · New Deal · Bank Holidays

Family _____ Friends _____

Homes _____ Pets _____ Cars _____

Jobs _____ Education _____

Medical History _____

1934

President Franklin D Roosevelt · Shirley Temple · John Dillinger

Family _____ Friends _____

Homes _____ Pets _____ Cars _____

Jobs _____ Education _____

Medical History _____

PERSONAL CHRONOLOGY

President Franklin D Roosevelt · Dust Bowl · Social Security · Big Bands **1935**

Family   Friends

Homes   Pets   Cars

Jobs   Education

Medical History

President Franklin D Roosevelt · Duke of Windsor and Mrs Simpson **1936**

Family   Friends

Homes   Pets   Cars

Jobs   Education

Medical History

President Franklin D Roosevelt · *Hindenburg* · Amelia Earhart Disappears **1937**

Family   Friends

Homes   Pets   Cars

Jobs   Education

Medical History

President Franklin D Roosevelt · Trapp Family Singers · Joe Louis **1938**

Family   Friends

Homes   Pets   Cars

Jobs   Education

Medical History

President Franklin D Roosevelt · World War II · *Gone with the Wind* **1939**

Family   Friends

Homes   Pets   Cars

Jobs   Education

Medical History

PERSONAL CHRONOLOGY

1940
President Franklin D Roosevelt · Dunkirk · Blitzkrieg · London Blitz

Family   Friends

Homes   Pets   Cars

Jobs   Education

Medical History

1941
President Franklin D Roosevelt · Pearl Harbor · US Enters World War II

Family   Friends

Homes   Pets   Cars

Jobs   Education

Medical History

1942
President Franklin D Roosevelt · War in Africa and Pacific

Family   Friends

Homes   Pets   Cars

Jobs   Education

Medical History

1943
President Franklin D Roosevelt · Italy Surrenders · Guadalcanal

Family   Friends

Homes   Pets   Cars

Jobs   Education

Medical History

1944
Presidents Franklin D Roosevelt and Harry S Truman · D Day

Family   Friends

Homes   Pets   Cars

Jobs   Education

Medical History

PERSONAL CHRONOLOGY

President Harry S Truman · A-Bomb! · VE Day · VJ Day · War Over			**1945**
Family		Friends	
Homes	Pets	Cars	
Jobs		Education	
Medical History			

President Truman · United Nations · Nuremberg War Crime Trials			**1946**
Family		Friends	
Homes	Pets	Cars	
Jobs		Education	
Medical History			

President Harry S Truman · The Marshall Plan · Jackie Robinson · Kon Tiki			**1947**
Family		Friends	
Homes	Pets	Cars	
Jobs		Education	
Medical History			

President Harry S Truman · Transistor · Israel · Cold War · Gandhi			**1948**
Family		Friends	
Homes	Pets	Cars	
Jobs		Education	
Medical History			

President Harry S Truman · NATO · Mao and Chiang Kai-shek in China			**1949**
Family		Friends	
Homes	Pets	Cars	
Jobs		Education	
Medical History			

1950

President Harry S Truman · Korean War-Inchon · Brinks Robbery

Family .... Friends ....

Homes .... Pets .... Cars ....

Jobs .... Education ....

Medical History ....

1951

President Harry S Truman · Korean War · MacArthur · Coast-to-Coast TV

Family .... Friends ....

Homes .... Pets .... Cars ....

Jobs .... Education ....

Medical History ....

1952

President Harry S Truman · Ike Visits Korea · England Gets A-Bomb

Family .... Friends ....

Homes .... Pets .... Cars ....

Jobs .... Education ....

Medical History ....

1953

President Dwight D Eisenhower · Korean Armistice · Hillary on Everest

Family .... Friends ....

Homes .... Pets .... Cars ....

Jobs .... Education ....

Medical History ....

1954

President Dwight D Eisenhower · Baby Boom · Polio Vaccine

Family .... Friends ....

Homes .... Pets .... Cars ....

Jobs .... Education ....

Medical History ....

PERSONAL CHRONOLOGY

President Dwight D Eisenhower · Rock and Roll · Disneyland Opens

1955

Family   Friends

Homes   Pets   Cars

Jobs   Education

Medical History

President Dwight D Eisenhower · Suez Canal Crisis · *Peyton Place*—Book

1956

Family   Friends

Homes   Pets   Cars

Jobs   Education

Medical History

President Dwight D Eisenhower · *Sputnik* · European Common Market

1957

Family   Friends

Homes   Pets   Cars

Jobs   Education

Medical History

President Dwight D Eisenhower · Space Race · Elvis Joins Army

1958

Family   Friends

Homes   Pets   Cars

Jobs   Education

Medical History

President Dwight D Eisenhower · Alaska and Hawaii Become States

1959

Family   Friends

Homes   Pets   Cars

Jobs   Education

Medical History

1960

President Dwight D Eisenhower · U-2 Spy Plane · *The Twist* · Ted Williams

Family   Friends

Homes   Pets   Cars

Jobs   Education

Medical History

1961

President John F Kennedy · Berlin Wall · Man in Space · Bay of Pigs

Family   Friends

Homes   Pets   Cars

Jobs   Education

Medical History

1962

President John F Kennedy · Cuban Missile Crisis · John Glen in Space

Family   Friends

Homes   Pets   Cars

Jobs   Education

Medical History

1963

Presidents John F Kennedy and Lyndon Johnson · JFK Dies in Dallas

Family   Friends

Homes   Pets   Cars

Jobs   Education

Medical History

1964

President Lyndon Johnson · Gulf of Tonkin · Zip Codes · Beatles

Family   Friends

Homes   Pets   Cars

Jobs   Education

Medical History

PERSONAL CHRONOLOGY

President Lyndon Johnson • Space Walk • Watts Riots • Warren Report   **1965**

Family   Friends

Homes   Pets   Cars

Jobs   Education

Medical History

President Johnson • Space Race • Vietnam Heats Up • Indira Gandhi   **1966**

Family   Friends

Homes   Pets   Cars

Jobs   Education

Medical History

President Lyndon Johnson • Superbowl I • 6 Day War • Summer of Love   **1967**

Family   Friends

Homes   Pets   Cars

Jobs   Education

Medical History

President Lyndon Johnson • TET Offensive • King and RFK Assassinations   **1968**

Family   Friends

Homes   Pets   Cars

Jobs   Education

Medical History

President Richard M Nixon • Men on Moon • Woodstock • Altamont   **1969**

Family   Friends

Homes   Pets   Cars

Jobs   Education

Medical History

PERSONAL CHRONOLOGY

1970

President Richard M Nixon • Kent State • Monday Night Football

Family   Friends

Homes   Pets   Cars

Jobs   Education

Medical History

1971

President Richard M Nixon • Voting Age 18 • Hot Pants • DB Cooper

Family   Friends

Homes   Pets   Cars

Jobs   Education

Medical History

1972

President Richard Nixon • Mark Spitz 7 Gold Medals • Nixon Visits China

Family   Friends

Homes   Pets   Cars

Jobs   Education

Medical History

1973

President Richard Nixon • Vietnam Over! • Gas Shortage • Free Agents

Family   Friends

Homes   Pets   Cars

Jobs   Education

Medical History

1974

Presidents Richard Nixon and Gerald Ford • Nixon Resigns • Patty Hearst

Family   Friends

Homes   Pets   Cars

Jobs   Education

Medical History

PERSONAL CHRONOLOGY

		1975
President Gerald Ford • Patty Hearst • Jimmy Hoffa • USS *Mayaguez*		
Family	Friends	
Homes	Pets	Cars
Jobs	Education	
Medical History		

		1976
President Gerald Ford • Bicentennial • Raid on Entebbe • Swine Flu		
Family	Friends	
Homes	Pets	Cars
Jobs	Education	
Medical History		

		1977
President Jimmy Carter • *Star Wars* • Elvis Dies • Disco • Son of Sam		
Family	Friends	
Homes	Pets	Cars
Jobs	Education	
Medical History		

		1978
President Jimmy Carter • Camp David Accord • Test Tube Babies		
Family	Friends	
Homes	Pets	Cars
Jobs	Education	
Medical History		

		1979
President Jimmy Carter • Three Mile Island • Afghanistan • Nicaragua		
Family	Friends	
Homes	Pets	Cars
Jobs	Education	
Medical History		

1980

President Jimmy Carter · US Hockey Team · ABSCAM · John Lennon

Family		Friends	
Homes	Pets		Cars
Jobs		Education	
Medical History			

1981

President Ronald Reagan · Hostages Free · Baseball Strike · President Shot

Family		Friends	
Homes	Pets		Cars
Jobs		Education	
Medical History			

1982

President Ronald Reagan · Falkland Islands · Football Strike · DeLorean

Family		Friends	
Homes	Pets		Cars
Jobs		Education	
Medical History			

1983

President Ronald Reagan · Korean Airliner · Beirut · America's Cup

Family		Friends	
Homes	Pets		Cars
Jobs		Education	
Medical History			

1984

President Ronald Reagan · Baby Fae · SDI · Famine in Africa

Family		Friends	
Homes	Pets		Cars
Jobs		Education	
Medical History			

PERSONAL CHRONOLOGY

President Ronald Reagan · Contras · Mexico City · AIDS

1985

Family   Friends

Homes   Pets   Cars

Jobs   Education

Medical History

President Ronald Reagan · Space Shuttle · Chernobyl · Marcos

1986

Family   Friends

Homes   Pets   Cars

Jobs   Education

Medical History

President Ronald Reagan · Jessica McClure · Madonna · Ollie North

1987

Family   Friends

Homes   Pets   Cars

Jobs   Education

Medical History

President Ronald Reagan · Fax Machines · Pan Am Flight 103

1988

Family   Friends

Homes   Pets   Cars

Jobs   Education

Medical History

President George Bush · Earthquake · Cold War · Panama · China

1989

Family   Friends

Homes   Pets   Cars

Jobs   Education

Medical History

1990

Family   Friends

Homes   Pets   Cars

Jobs   Education

Medical History

1991

Family   Friends

Homes   Pets   Cars

Jobs   Education

Medical History

1992

Family   Friends

Homes   Pets   Cars

Jobs   Education

Medical History

1993

Family   Friends

Homes   Pets   Cars

Jobs   Education

Medical History

1994

Family   Friends

Homes   Pets   Cars

Jobs   Education

Medical History

PERSONAL CHRONOLOGY

1995

Family   Friends

Homes   Pets   Cars

Jobs   Education

Medical History

1996

Family   Friends

Homes   Pets   Cars

Jobs   Education

Medical History

1997

Family   Friends

Homes   Pets   Cars

Jobs   Education

Medical History

1998

Family   Friends

Homes   Pets   Cars

Jobs   Education

Medical History

1999

Family   Friends

Homes   Pets   Cars

Jobs   Education

Medical History

PERSONAL CHRONOLOGY FOR THE YEAR 2000·

JANUARY _____
_____

FEBRUARY _____
_____

MARCH _____
_____

APRIL _____
_____

MAY _____
_____

JUNE _____
_____

JULY _____
_____

AUGUST _____
_____

SEPTEMBER _____
_____

OCTOBER _____
_____

NOVEMBER _____
_____

DECEMBER _____
_____

20 TH
CENTURY
INDEX

PERSONAL MILESTONES

_____

_____

_____

_____

_____

_____

_____

_____

_____

_____

_____

_____

_____

_____

_____

_____

_____

_____

_____

_____

_____

_____

_____

_____

_____

_____

_____

_____

_____

LIFELOG 20TH CENTURY INDEX

This is an index of the entries in LIFELOG. Ours is a culture fascinated by firsts, facts, and figures. In LIFELOG items have been chosen to help the readers/writers remember a time in their lives. Some items are listed when they first appeared and others when they became popular. After each letter there are lines and blank spaces if you wish to make entries in the index as well as the years and the chronology.

_____

_____

_____

_____

_____

_____

_____

_____

_____

A

B

C

Curse of the Cat People—Movie 1944 Movies
Curtis, Tony—Actor 1961 Nov
Cyclamates—Product 1969 Jun
Cyrano de Bergerac—Theater 1947 Dec

———————————————————
———————————————————
———————————————————
———————————————————
———————————————————
———————————————————
———————————————————

D

DC-7—Airplane 1953 Jul
DC-10—Airplane 1989 Jul
D-Day—War 1944 H-lines,
 1944 Jun
DDT—News 1939
 1972 Dec
DEW Line—Radar 1954 Sep
DMZ Korea—War 1953 Jan
DMZ Vietnam—War 1972 Mar
Da Doo Ron Ron—Song 1977 Jul
Da Vinci, Leonardo—Art 1967 Feb
Da Ya Think I'm Sexy—Song 1979 Feb
Daddy—Music 1941 Jun
Dalai Lama—Religon 1959 H-lines
Daley, Richard—Politics 1955 Nov
Daley, Richard, Jr—Politics 1989 Apr
Dalkon Shield—News 1987 Dec
Dallas (1978-)—Television 1980 H-lines
Damn Yankees—Theater 1955 Apr

Dan Patch—Horse Racing 1902
Dancing in the Street—Song 1964 Oct
Dancing Machine—Song 1974 May
Dancing on the Ceiling—Song 1986 Songs
Dancing Queen—Song 1977 Mar
Daniloff, Nick—News 1986 Sep
Danskins—Product 1979 Apr
Dark Half—Book 1989 Books
Dark Lady—Song 1974 Mar
Dark Star—Race Horse 1953 May
Darkness at Noon—Book 1941 Jul
Dating Game, The (1966-1970)—Television
 1965 Dec
Datsun—Automobile 1980 May
Davis Cup—Tennis 1900
Davis, Angela—Activist 1972 Jun
Davis, Ernie—Football 1961 Oct
Davis, Major Gen Ben—News 1959 May
Davy Crockett—Television 1954 Dec,
 1955 May
Day After, The—Television 1983 Nov
Day Dream Believer—Song 1967 Dec
Day for Night—Movie 1973 Jun
Day in the Life of America, A—Book 1986 Books
Day of the Jackal, The—Movie 1971 Books
Day of the Locust—Book 1939
Day the Earth Stood Still, The—Movie
 1951 Movies
Day, Doris—Actress 1961 Nov,
 1948 Mar, 1961 Nov
Daylight Savings—News 1966 H-lines,
 1942 Feb
Days of Heaven—Movie 1978 Movies
Days of Wine and Roses—Movie 1962 Nov
Dazzle—Book 1990 Books
De Gaulle, Charles—News 1944 Aug,
 1958 H-lines
De Mille, Cecil B—Movies 1924
De Soto—Automobile 1952 Oct,
 1956 Jul
Dead Poets Society—Movie 1989 Movies

E

F

F Troop (1965-1967)—Television
                                    1965 May
FAA—Business   1958 May
FAX Machines—Business   1988 H-lines
FBI—News   1924,
        1950 Mar, 1970 Feb, 1989 Aug
FCC—Radio   1961 Jul
FDA—Business   1967 Apr
Face in the Crowd, A—Movie   1957 Movies
Face the Music—Television   1948 Dec
Fail Safe—Movie   1964 Sep
Fairbanks, Douglas—Actor   1925
Faith—Album—Song   1987 Dec
Falcon and the Snowman—Movie 1985 Aug
Falcon Crest (1981-)—Television
                                    1984 Mar
Falkland Island War—War   1982 H-lines,
                                    1982 Apr
Fall of Paris, The—Book   1941 May
Falwell, Jerry—News   1987 Sep
Fame—Song   1975 Songs
Fame—Movie   1980 Jun
Family Affair—Song   1971 Songs
Family Affair (1966-1971)—Television
                                    1967 Jun
Family Pictures—Book   1990 May
Famous Amos—Cookies   1976 Feb
Fantasia—Movie   1940 Mar
Far Pavillions, The—Book   1978 Jul
Farewell My Lovely—Book   1940 Books
Farm Aid Concert—Music   1985 Sep
Farmer's Daughter, The—Movie 1947 Jul
Farouk, King—News   1952 H-lines
Fast Car—Song   1988 Songs
Father Divine—Religion   1919
Father Knows Best (1954-1963)—Television
                                    1958 Nov
Father of the Bride—Movie   1950 Movies

Fatherhood—Book   1986 Books
Faubus, Orville, Gov—Politics   1958 Sep
Fawcett, Farrah—Fashion   1977 Nov
Fear of Flying—Book   1973 Dec
Feels So Good—Song   1978 May
Feller, Bob—Baseball   1951 Jul
Felt Tip Pen—Product   1960 Aug
Feminine Mystique, The—Book 1963 Books
Fergie—News   1986 Jul
Ferraro, Geraldine—Politics   1984 Jul,
                                    1984 Oct
Ferrer, José—Actor   1947 Dec
Fever—Song   1958 Songs
Few Minutes with Andy Rooney, A—Book
                                    1982 Books
Fibber McGee & Molly—Radio   1940 Feb
Field of Dreams—Movie   1989 Movies
Fields, WC—Actor   1941 Nov
Filmore Theater—Music   1970 Jun
Fingertips Part 2—Song   1963 Jul
Finley, Charlie—Baseball   1973 Dec
Fiorello—Theater   1959 Oct
Fire—Song   1975 Jan
Fire—Song   1979 Mar
Fire and Rain—Song   1970 Dec
Fireside Cookbook, The—Book   1949 Books
Firestarter—Book   1980 Books
Firestone Tires—Product   1988 Feb
Fischer, Bobby—Chess   1960 Dec,
                                    1972 Sep
Fish Ties—Fad   1986 Mar
Fisher, Eddie—Actor   1954 Sep
Fistful of Dollars, A—Movie   1967 Mar
Fit for Life—Book   1986 Feb
Five Easy Pieces—Movie   1970 Mar
Flag Burning—Politics   1989 Jul
Flappers—Fad   1919
Flashbulbs—Product   1951 Dec
Flashdance—Movie   1983 Aug
Fleming, Peggy—Skating   1968 Feb
Flight of the Phoenix, The—Movie 1966 Dec

G

LIFELOG 20TH CENTURY INDEX

H

I

J

K

N

LifeLog 20th Century Index

P

Q

R

LifeLog 20th Century Index

S

LifeLog 20th Century Index

T

TV—Television	1948 Nov, 1951 H-lines
TV Dinners—Product	1960 Jul
TV Guide—Magazine	1953 Apr
Tab—Product	1963 May
Tacoma Bridge—News	1940 Nov
Taft, William Howard—Politics	1908, 1910, 1912
Taft-Hartley Act—News	1947 H-lines, 1947 Jun
Tai-Pan—Book	1966 Books
Taj Mahal—Hotel	1990 Apr
Take It to the Limit—Song	1976 Mar
Take Me Home Country Road—Song	1971 Songs
Take Me Out to the Ball Game—Song	1908
Take the "A" Train—Song	1941 Songs
Taking a Chance on Love—Song	1940 Songs
Tales of the South Pacific—Book	1947 Books
Talmadge, Norma—Actress	1924
Tammy—Song	1957 May
Tango Argentino—Theater	1985 Dec
Taos—News	1969 Dec
Tapestry—Album	1971 Jun
Taps—Movie	1982 Nov
Tarkenton, Fran—Football	1974 Oct
Tarzan of the Apes—Book	1914
Taxi (1978-1983)—Television	1980 Feb
Taxi Driver—Movie	1976 May
Taylor, James—Music	1971 Jul
Taylor, Jim—Football	1962 Dec
Taylor, Liz—Actress	1961 Nov
Taylor, Robert—Actor	1942 Movies
Tea and Sympathy—Theater	1953 May
Tea for Two—Song	1924
Teach Me Tonight—Song	1954 Songs
Teachings of Don Juan, The—Book	1968 Books
Teamsters—News	1957 Dec
Teapot Dome Oil—News	1923
Tears of a Clown—Song	1970 Dec
Ted Mack Original Amateur Hour (1948-1960)—Television	1948 Jan
Teddy Bears—Product	1902
Teddy Ruxpin—Product	1985 Dec
Teen Angel—Song	1960 May
Teenage Mutant Ninja Turtles—Movie	1990 Movies
Teenager in Love, A—Song	1959 Songs
Teflon—Product	1948 Apr
Telephone Booth Stuffing—Fad	1952 Aug
Telephone Company Deregulation—Business	1982 Jan
Telstar—Song	1962 Dec
Ten Commandments, The—Movie	1956 Movies
Tender Mercies—Movie	1983 Movies
Tender Trap, The—Movie	1955 Sep
Tennessee Waltz—Song	1950 Songs
Tequila—Song	1958 Songs
Terkel, Studs—Writer	1974 Mar
Terminator—Movie	1984 Dec
Terms of Endearment—Movie	1983 Nov
Test Tube Baby—News	1978 H-lines
TET Offensive—War	1968 H-lines
Texas Instruments—Product	1971 Aug
Thalidomide Babies—News	1962 H-lines, 1962 Aug
Thank God I'm a Country Boy—Song	1975 Jun
That Girl (1966-1971)—Television	1967 Jun
That Lucky Old Sun—Song	1949 Songs
That Man from Rio—Movie	1965 Jun
That Old Black Magic—Song	1942 Jul
That Old Gal of Mine—Song	1912
That'll Be the Day—Song	1958 Songs
That's Amore—Song	1954 Oct
That's Incredible (1980-1984)—Television	1980 Sep

U

Coming from AnDex 2000™ : LIFELOG™ , 1950-2050, an
Arts LIFELOG™ 1900-2000, a Sports LIFELOG™ , and
LIFELOGS™ to cover a variety of subjects and time periods.

To contact AnDex 2000™ about LIFELOG™ updates, other
LIFELOG™ products, or to get on our mailing list, please
write to:

> AnDex 2000™
> 9188 W Pico, Suite 112
> Los Angeles, Ca 90035